A Small Cog

The Story of Montfortebeek Flight,
3 Commando Brigade Air Squadron
Royal Marines in the 1982 campaign to recapture the
Falkland Islands.

ISBN 978-1-908123-23-7

First Published in 2021 by the
Royal Marines Historical Society
National Museum of the Royal Navy
Her Majesty's Naval Base (PP66)
Portsmouth
Hampshire
PO1 3NH

Printed and bound in Great Britain by Printchamps.co.uk

A Small Cog

The Story of Montfortebeek Flight,
3 Commando Brigade Air Squadron
Royal Marines in the 1982 campaign
to recapture the Falkland Islands.

By Nick Pounds

Royal Marines Historical Society
Special Publication 51
Series Editor John Rawlinson

List of Illustrations

Contents

Maps

Foreword
Peter Cameron MC
Then Major Peter Cameron RM: San Carlos 1982

I am immensely proud to be asked to write the foreword to this story of Montfortebeek Flight, 3 Commando Brigade Air Squadron Royal Marines in the campaign to recapture the Falkland Islands - OPERATION CORPORATE - appropriately titled 'A Small Cog'. The idea was first conceived at our Squadron's 35th Anniversary Reunion of the Falklands War, held at Pangbourne College on the 21st May 2017, exactly 35 years to the day after the landings in San Carlos Water.

The painting below is one of several commissioned for a book entitled "Crossing the Grey Line", by Rick Jolly, the commander of 3 Commando Brigade's Medical Squadron for the campaign, which sadly, he did not live to complete. I am now the proud owner of the painting. Rick's intention had been to describe the various casualty evacuation rescues he took part in that day, flying in the back of a naval Wessex helicopter, which had included the extraction of two of three casualties from C Flight,

First Light, San Carlos Water by D R Hardstaff

who we lost tragically on the morning of 'D' Day. The painting shows Gazelle 'CX' in the foreground, about to escort a Sea King with an underslung load of Mortar Ammunition destined for of 42 Commando RM at Port San Carlos. As you will read in more detail, a retreating enemy party shot at both aircraft, hitting the Gazelle, and narrowly missing the Sea King, whose crewman reported the incident to the Combined Amphibious Headquarters (HQ) on board HMS Fearless. The initial 'follow up' aircraft was Gazelle 'CY', shown in the background of the picture, which, unbeknown to us, was in turn shot down by the same retreating enemy. M Flight, in reserve, was then committed to action for the first time, to follow up on this incident and find out what had happened.

When the Argentineans invaded the Falklands on Friday 2nd April 1982, I judged my Squadron to be generally in good shape and ready for war. We had just completed a major NATO, Arctic Exercise in North Norway, for all the Scout crews and technicians and, at the same time, mountain flying and fighter evasion training in the Scottish Highlands for all the Gazelle aircrew; we just needed to tweak the edges a bit. The eloquent description that follows, drawing on their collective memory, tells how M Flight achieved this, and can be taken to represent what was going on throughout the Squadron.

When I committed the Squadron to 'action' in the early hours of 'D' Day, on the 21st May 1982, as we were crossing the 'grey line' from ship to shore' so to speak, into the unknown, into the unexpected and soon to be into real danger, the tension in my HQ and in each cockpit was palpable. Thereafter, the shock of our losses on 'D' Day, so early in the landing, were felt right through the Brigade and beyond.

As a result, the Squadron was on tenterhooks for the next few days, as we went about the duty of supporting our Brigade during the Battle for San Carlos Water. However, what we were to do next proved to be relatively far more serious. M Flight, together with two Scout aircraft from B Flight, were to be in direct support of 2 Para for their assault on Darwin and Goose Green. To the best of my knowledge, this was the first time that light helicopters had been used to support a UK infantry battalion in a conventional war setting; we had to get it right. So, the Squadron's Senior Pilot, Andrew Eames, was placed forward, with the 2 Para HQ, to coordinate all our tasking in their support. M Flight tell us the gripping story, including the circumstances surrounding the tragic loss of Scout 'DR' and what action they took at the time.

After the battle it was concluded that; 'The work of Andrew Eames as the 3 BAS Aviation Liaison Officer forward at Battalion Headquarters in the heat of the battle proved invaluable. The small battlefield utility helicopters flown by military aviators had proven their worth in support of the land battle. Their magnificent working in support was instrumental in 2 Para's glorious victory; also, countless lives were saved. and 2 Para's doctor was heard to say of the 3 BAS support, 'They were wonderful. Just when you thought 'God I really need a helicopter now', there it would be, coming over some fold in the ground. They were the bravest of anyone. Superb. Like the Seventh Cavalry. They kept on coming....' [1]

After that action, M Flight went on to support 3 Para in their Battle for Longdon, 45 Cdo RM in their Battle for Two Sisters and 2 Para again, with a Troop of Blues & Royals under their command, in their Battle for Wireless Ridge on the last night of the war, amongst other supporting tasks. What a magnificent achievement it was; all tasks were completed with such determination and also without further loss to the Squadron.

The skill and proficiency of the aircrew and those who supported them, both on the decks en-route to the Falklands, and on the ground once we got there, were quite remarkable. All should be highly commended for their combined efforts and determination to succeed, both in the initial amphibious stages, when they were first committed to battle at San Carlos Water in a hostile air environment, and thereafter in the subsequent land battles, starting with that for Darwin and Goose Green and in other actions that they supported during that War. Bravo Zulu![2]

In conclusion, I cannot praise Nick Pounds and all the ranks of M Flight and their families enough for bringing to the Squadron, and others who may be close to it, an opportunity to relive what it was like all those years ago through this delightful and gripping story of the Falklands War. For me, and I am certain for others, the wheel is still turning!

Finally, I cannot do no better than to quote our commander at the time, Julian Thompson, who wrote of the Squadron:

Without our light helicopters many of the young men alive today would be dead, many of our attacks would have foundered for lack of ammunition and the campaign would have taken longer to win - if indeed, given the close-run thing that it was, it could be won at all. The light helicopter, flown by brave, skilled aircrew proved itself in battle during Operation Corporate. The service given to units was superb. They really were the bravest of anyone.[3]

Nick Pounds and others from his team paint a graphic, personal and extremely detailed picture what is like to be in a front-line aviation sub-unit, operating light battlefield helicopters in an old fashioned conventional war, both from violently pitching flight decks in the South Atlantic and from field locations ashore, in a hostile air environment, the first British and, indeed, Western helicopter aircrew to find themselves in this situation since helicopters were brought into service. Their story tells also of life back home for the families, and their concerns and feelings, as they heard of events as the War unfolded.

You will read how M Flight diligently and most professionally grappled with the challenges set, notably: the designing and fitting a GPMG mount to the aircraft; the fitting

---

[1] Army Air Corps Journal 1983 - OPERATION CORPORATE 3 Commando Brigade Air Squadron
[2] Bravo Zulu: The NATO Signal Book's 2-letter signal group meaning Well Done... (Jolly 1999: p61)
[3] Op cit - Army Air Corps Journal

Port San Carlos Memorial

Camilla Creek Memorial

of and firing newly acquired SNEB rockets and flying with first generation Passive Night Goggles (PNG) both for the first time. These evolutions were not without some hairy and extremely frightening moments, (including with yours truly!), as you will read. M Flight were the first flight in the Squadron to be online to fly with PNG and they tell the remarkable story of some 17 missions they achieved flying with this equipment saving, countless lives and resupplying crucial stores at night, direct to the front line. The pilots deservedly were duly awarded for their superb endeavours.

The final chapter of the story tells of remembering lost comrades during the voyage home. Two fine Squadron memorials have subsequently been erected in honour of those lost comrades. For those who we lost on the first day, Ken Francis, Andy Evans and Brett Giffin, a memorial now stands Port San Carlos and for Richard Nunn DFC, lost during the battle for Goose Green, another fine memorial now stands at Camilla Creek. We will remember them.

Preface

This is the story of Montfortebeek (M) Flight – the last Royal Marines Air Troop having its last "Hurrah!"– when it took part in the campaign to retake the Falkland Islands, at the time when I had the privilege to be the Flight Commander. This short story started as a personal endeavour, to record a few notes against the possibility that my grandchildren might one day ask: "What did Grandpa do in the war?" My first draft was shaped by my reliable but exceedingly bland flying logbook and (38 years after the event) by my exceedingly unreliable but colourful memory, drawing upon some of the many, excellent books and articles concerning this conflict, to provide both a wider context and a measure of control. However, at a reunion of 3 Commando Brigade Air Squadron (3 BAS), of which M Flight was but one small part, it became clear that there were many others who might wish also to have some record. So, I have undertaken that my final duty as the last commander of M Flight should be to write this story, which includes the experiences of as many members of the Flight to whom I could reach out, so long after the event.

This is not a comprehensive view of the Falkland Island's Campaign but rather, an account of how it looked to a tiny group of us who were just 'a small cog' in that vast enterprise. However, our tale will, necessarily, refer to the major evolutions of the campaign, since they shaped the events in which we became directly engaged. At that time, a light aviation squadron was different to most other military units. Conducting missions that ranged across the Task Force, engaging with Brigade HQ, ferrying senior officers, working with individual units and monitoring their command nets, the aircrew enjoyed a unique and unparalleled insight into the unfolding story, probably far greater than most others , who rarely left the confines of their own units or headquarters. However, the aircrew would have been helpless without the team of engineers and supporting 'ground crew' who looked after them and their aircraft, often in atrocious conditions and usually with scant knowledge of what was unfolding around them; this account, I hope, also gives some credit to their efforts, bravery and experiences.

People looking back from some point in the future, may wonder how it was that 3 BAS went to war with the anomalous structure of A, B, C and M Flights. It is not my place to rehearse the history of that fine Squadron – others have made an excellent job of that.[4] Here, I wish simply to explain why things were as they were at that time. The process of moving from five loosely affiliated air troops (each linked to a unit of 3

---

[4] See Bancroft (1973) and Reece (2012) for the full Story

Commando Brigade and named after one of that unit's battle honours) into a cohesive Squadron structure was well underway but not quite completed. Brunei, Dieppe, Salerno and Kangaw Flights had reformed into A and C Flights (Gazelle) and B Flight (Scout), each to be 6 aircraft. M Flight, affiliated to 45 Commando in distant Arbroath, was all that remained of the old structure, though its days were numbered. My primary task, on assignment, was to prepare for its amalgamation in the autumn of 1982. As it happened, the old, 3 aircraft, structure of the air troops perfectly fitted a key logistic constraint of this campaign. The maximum capacity of the small decks allocated to transport the Gazelles was three aircraft, so we were committed to battle as M Flight, whilst A and C deployed with reduced numbers.

As the holder of the pen, the narrative is predominantly written from my perspective but I hope that I have, adequately included the memories, and stories of other members of that magnificent team, to properly reflect the contribution they made to the citation awarded to the whole Squadron after the campaign:

> *From the first landings in San Carlos Water on 21 May until the Argentine Surrender 3 Commando Brigade Air Squadron RM supported the landing forces often under appalling conditions, by day and night and in the early stages, frequently attacked Argentine fighter and ground attack aircraft.*
>
> *During the initial landings and in the course of the attack on Darwin and Goose Green the Squadron lost 3 aircraft to enemy action together with 4 aircrew killed and 2 wounded.*
>
> *The Squadron was involved in every major battle during the campaign in a variety of roles: reconnaissance, liaison, the movement of ammunition to the front line and the recovery of casualties from forward positions.*
>
> *All these were undertaken in a variety of weather conditions, sometimes at night and often under fire.*
>
> *Its 6 Scout and 9 Gazelle helicopters flew a total of 2,110 hours in just over 3 weeks reflecting a remarkable rate of serviceability and flying.*
>
> *The courage and skill of the aircrew backed by the skill and devotion to duty of the ground support enabled the Squadron to make a significant contribution to the defeat of the Argentine ground forces and their surrender on 14 June.*

Finally, before embarking on our story, I must warn that it is reliant in large measure on the failing memories and "oft' told stories" of aging Royal Marines and we all know what that means!

The Team

We were a mixed bunch and, with a couple of exceptions, relatively inexperienced when it came to aviation. Among the pilots, Bill O'Brien was probably the most air experienced; whilst he had only 590 pilot flying hours, he had been an air gunner for nearly 3 years, before training as a pilot. Even I, as Flight Commander, had only 600 flying hours to my credit! Will Scott, the second in command, had joined the Flight in January, straight from pilot training. Even less experienced was Terry Waldron, who joined straight from pilot training as were about to embark. Fortunately we were joined en-route by a Grenadier Guards Sergeant, Angus Horswill, who had been about to return to the Army after a three year attachment with 3 BAS, but who had succeeded in persuading the system to let him stay for the forthcoming operation. His total of 850 hours from made the late arrival the most experienced pilot in the flight! Among the five observers, we were lucky to have a couple of seasoned sergeants, 'JC' Woods and Ken Priest but the others were relatively new to the game. Our nine aircraft maintainers were from the Army, a Royal Electrical and Mechanical Engineers (REME) Light Aid Detachment (LAD). As a detached flight, we were lucky to have an experienced Artificer Sergeant Major (ASM), John Hopkinson, heading the LAD as well as a long serving sergeant, Charlie Walker. We had a general duties Sergeant, Ian Mellor, responsible for administration, three marine signallers three aircraft ground handlers, and three Drivers, all marines bar one, Naval Airman Kirkland, who was the only one among them who had ever worked on a ships deck before! One of the Marines, Donaldson, had been declared too young to go with the Flight on operations in Northern Ireland a few months earlier but was, it seemed, eligible to remain for what was potentially a full blown conventional war!

Our three Gazelle aircraft were registered as XZ380, XX413 and XX376. However, we routinely referred to them by their callsign, following the Fleet Air Arm (FAA), two letter system for quick recognition- the first letter denoting aircraft type, whilst the second was the large letter painted on each aircraft. Thus, throughout this narrative I refer to them, as we did at the time, as CM, CZ, and CK respectively.

M Flight on the Way Home

Woods Horswill O'Brien Unknown Davenport Waldron Carter Stanford Hopkinson
Priest Scott Walker Woodhouse Donaldson Drummond Kirkland Tribe Condron Parker Mellor Pounds
Walkinshaw J. Mackenzie Urey D. Mackenzie Roberts Cooper Hamilton Stuart

Off to War: Embarkation

For M Flight, it all began rather unexpectedly on Friday 2nd April, the day we were due to commence our Easter leave. In distant Arbroath, we were vaguely aware of events in the South Atlantic - Argentinian scrap metal dealers on South Georgia and suspicious naval evolutions near to the Falkland Islands – but we were not aware of the plans that were evolving in London. I was woken at five o'clock that morning, to be told that a unit recall was underway and to report immediately to 45 Commando's HQ to attend an 'orders group' (O Gp). This abrupt awakening happened to coincide with a power cut that had caused a blackout and my initial, befuddled thoughts were that this was, either a late April Fool joke in very poor taste, or that WWIII had started! Andrew Whitehead, the commanding officer (CO), quickly outlined the real situation and informed us that 3 Commando Brigade had been placed under orders to embark within 72 hours, absence of notice to move notwithstanding, as part of a Naval Task Force that was being assembled to retake the Falkland Islands.

As evidence of our lack of awareness, JC Woods, living with his family in council housing in Arbroath, was missed by the unit recall procedure. He was still unaware what was happening when his father phoned him to ask if he had heard the news; JC replied that he had but that it would not really affect him; he was still planning to drive south with his wife and children later that day, to attend a family wedding in Cambridgeshire. His father's reply was uncannily accurate; he said, "I think you will be heading further south than you think"!

Returning from the O Gp and after a brief telephone conversation with the Squadron's Senior Pilot, Andrew Eames, I briefed the assembled flight on the situation and preparations required by us. The first task for them was to pack personal kit for a deployment in the South Atlantic and tell their families what was happening.

Dave (Monster) Mackenzie, one of our bowser operators, remembers the single men going back to support company accommodation,

> *Most of the lads hadn't even heard of the Falklands. The only reason I knew was due to the fact one of the lads when I was in Plymouth had upset the Sgt Major and got a draft there. He went into his office and kicked off about the fact he had put Scotland as an area to avoid on his draft chit. The Sgt Major had the last laugh pointing out it wasn't in Scotland!*

We were all of the same mind, that it was a late April fool. In the grot[5] we got our Bergens and filled them with anything we could find to bulk them out and make them look like they were packed. Kirky [NA Kirkland], came in the grot asking us what he needed to pack, when we told him your Bergen he said, "I don't have one"; "what have you got?" we asked, "a seaman's grip" he said, and we told him "well pack that!, we won't be going any place and you will be all ready to go on leave tomorrow"

These actions would come back to bite us later, when JC asked us to get our kit, as he had been instructed to do a kit inspection. JC was an accomplished soldier, [he had been] in a fighting company with 45 Commando prior to becoming air crew and we knew we wouldn't be able to pull the wool over his eyes. All sorts came out of our Bergen's pillows, sleeping bags etc. and Kirky with his seaman's grip! JC quite rightly had a sense of humour failure, but seeing the funny side he took the six marines to one side and pointed out that he expected better from us and we should be leading by example and to get round the inexperienced and attached ranks helping them to get the kit they required - this wasn't a bite. That day and evening was spent properly servicing and packing our kit. On Saturday morning we had a re-run and passed with flying colours.

The remainder of that first day was spent preparing and loading vehicles. Initially we were planning to take the LAD's 4-ton tool truck and 4 ton flatbed that was fitted with a HIAB[6] Crane, which would carry two containers of stores and aircraft spares; also a Land Rover fitted for radio (FFR) for our Command Post (CP). All the tools, spares, stores, etc. had been laid out in the hanger and loaded by mid-afternoon so, with no further orders for a move, I stood the Flight down, instructing them to report back the next day. By Saturday it had all changed, the only vehicle that we were being allowed to take was the FFR and its trailer. Everything we took would have to go in the FFR and trailer, and the two containers. This was a particular blow for Charlie Walker, who had fitted out the back of the tool truck as a workshop, with the addition of a bedroom, and kitchen, complete with a Burco boiler, generator, and space heater. As the saying goes, any fool can be uncomfortable in the field. The rest of Saturday was spent reloading the containers and FFR, trying to squeeze in the maximum amount of kit. As well as our own preparations, we were helping to facilitate the deployment of 45 Commando. Significantly, we flew Andrew Whitehead to RAF Leuchars, to catch a flight to Plymouth to meet the Brigade Commander; the first small leg of his long journey towards the capture of Mount 'Two Sisters', some three months later.

I think it fair to say that, young men as we were, most of us were elated at the prospect of doing what we had joined and trained for but, at the same time, many had concerns about the domestic impact of this sudden and unexpected development. For those with families living in Arbroath, having been prepared to depart on 2 April, there was the stress of saying goodbye each morning, only to have to repeat the whole thing the next day. JC recounts a typical experience:

---

[5] A ... room personalised by its owner... (Jolly, 1999: p205)
[6] HIAB: Finnish Hydrauliska Industry AktiBolag

My personal enthusiasm for going to war was not shared by my wife, Carolyn, as I eagerly climbed into the attic to retrieve my M&AW[7] kit. I grabbed the family car and headed back into work with my kit. On arrival, we started to pack the Flight vehicles and search for maps of the Falkland Islands. The vehicles were packed by about 15:00 and we were sent home but told to remain within the Arbroath area. The next morning, we 'turned to'[8] but, with not a lot for us to do, we were sent home again at lunchtime - same rules.

Those with families in the South were more concerned about disruption of their planned leave. Will Scott had only recently joined as the Flight 2i/c and had not moved his wife up to Arbroath, because we were scheduled shortly to deploy with 45 Commando on a long exercise in Canada, before moving to Plymouth in the Autumn. Easter leave had been expected to provide a welcome break to their separation. Terry Waldron had only just completed pilot training. He had been given a hasty Squadron acceptance check, which involved flying across southern England, under the scrutiny of the Squadron Qualified Helicopter Instructor (QHI),[9] to collect the Brigade's allocation of Falkland Islands maps, before being told to report to M Flight, as soon as possible. Having driven through the night, he decided to stop in Carnoustie, where his wife was staying with her parents. He had planned a late breakfast before continuing to Arbroath but, seeing two gazelles fly past, apparently heading south, thought it might be a good idea to get going. He kissed his wife goodbye and said he would be back later. Later turned out to be four months later! Personally, I had to work out how, in my absence, to re-consolidate my family, which at the time was about as stretched out as it could be; with wife, 2-year-old daughter and new-born baby son in Bury; car and dog in Arbroath; and house in Plymouth.

As an opinionated, 30 year old Royal Marines captain, studying for staff promotion exams, I thought that I knew a thing or two about international relations and, in order to help calm the fears of their families, informed the Flight that this was a classic example of a diplomatic storm in a teacup and that we were simply being mobilised to underpin diplomatic negotiations. I told them that the sooner we got ourselves ready to deploy, the sooner we would all be allowed to proceed on leave. After two days of hectic preparation, my assessment was beginning to look flawed when we received orders to embark on the Royal Fleet Auxiliary (RFA) Sir Percival, a landing ship logistic (LSL), at Marchwood Military Port in Southampton, by mid-day on Monday 5th April. Later, I was comforted somewhat to learn that, down in Plymouth, the rest of the Squadron had been given a similar story.

Most of the Flight, under the command of John Hopkinson, set off by road on 4th April, to join the ship that evening and prepare for arrival of the aircraft the following day. They were followed later by Monster and Dolly Drummond, one of the aircrew

---

[7] M&AW: Mountain and Arctic Warfare – we were heading into a possible Southern Hemisphere winter.
[8] Turn to: Start work (Jolly,1999 p 471)
[9] QHI is a qualification required to teach pilots to fly. Every Squadron has one officially appointed to facilitate and oversee the maintenance of necessary flying qualifications – which includes a Squadron Acceptance check

observers, in the FFR that was towing a trailer full of the LAD's tool's and anything else we had managed to squeeze in. The plan was that they would drive through the night to reach Marchwood at about the same time as the aircraft. However as Monster explains:

It soon become clear that it was going to be a long journey; the vehicle was way overloaded, and it struggled to get over 40mph. At crack of sparrow fart we ended up in Bath, tired and hungry. The vehicle was fitted out with all the signals kit, radios chargers etc, and the trailer was full of LAD kit. We parked the vehicle in a secure area, at the back of the local fire station, on the south side of the bridge in Bath city centre and went wandering around, with our SLRs slung over our shoulders, looking for a café but with no luck. On returning to the fire station the watch on duty took us in to the station made us a wet of tea and cooked us a full English. (never did get back there to thank them). It was going to be a close thing to get to the ship in time and I am not sure if we were late or just made it in time; the fact that the helicopters were late probably detracted from us.

Meanwhile, Angus Horswill, together with Ken Priest was preparing to join M Fl in CM, that had been with the Squadron LAD at Coypool. The plan was to rendezvous with the other two aircraft that were flying south at Middle Wallop, our final fuel stop before embarking. Angus's:

first problem was that I'd handed back all my kit to the QM and a visit to try and reclaim it found that the cupboard was bare. They didn't even have any 9mm pistols left and I was forced to accept an SMG which is not a very practical weapon for a Gazelle pilot. To add to that, I had to plan the flight and check on the state of my aircraft for an early departure the next day.

RFA Sir Percival

This unexpected and sudden turn of events came as a blow to Alyson Priest:

We lived in Plymstock near Plymouth, where Ken had joined me, our Old-English Sheepdog and eight month old baby girl at the end of March, after returning from nearly three months in Norway with B Flight and three more in Northern Ireland prior to that. We had expected to enjoy some leave together before Ken would have to return to M Flight at Arbroath, so it came as quite a surprise when on April 5th Ken announced he was flying not to Arbroath but to Middle Wallop with Angus Horswill, to meet M flight who were embarking for the voyage. Not living in married quarters and being remote from the other families I was left pretty much in the dark, with no information forthcoming except what we heard on the news. Where were the Falklands Islands anyway, somewhere off Scotland perhaps? Ken met his brother Derek at Middle Wallop, where he worked as a civilian engineer, and was able to tell him he might not make it to his forthcoming wedding!

To join Sir Percival by noon, with an estimated five hours flight time for the two aircraft in Arbroath, we had planned an early departure on 5th April but thick fog prevented our take off and it was mid-morning before it had burned off sufficiently for us safely to get airborne. Each aircraft carried two aircrew and one of the two REME technicians, who had stayed with, us, armed with a few essential tools, to ensure the aircraft could be persuaded to start. To make the quickest passage, we flew as a pair, down the spine of the country, using a combination of radar advisory and radar control air traffic services, with only a couple of fuel stops. The first was at RAF Leeming and the second at the Army Air Corps (AAC) Centre at Middle Wallop, where we were joined, for the rest of the journey, by Angus Horswill and Ken Priest in CM. The teams providing our fuel all assured us that we were 'lucky bastards' to be going to war, though we could not help but reflect that their enthusiasm to go to war seemed be inversely proportionate to the likelihood of them becoming involved! That said, Angus, having arrived at Middle Wallop ahead of the Scotland contingent, was seriously propositioned to swop places by Don Burton who had recently left M Flt in order to start a (then) highly coveted conversion course to the newly fielded Westland Lynx TOW!

Will Scott and I, who were flying together, nearly became the first casualties of the war somewhere in a hot blue haze 5,000 feet above the Midlands, when a combination of previous days of frantic activity, an early start, the monotony of our flight and the cosy warmth, caused me to doze off at the controls. Will must have been in a similar state or just assumed that I knew what I was doing, because he did not pick it up and it was only a strident call from the other aircraft that brought me back to consciousness in time to recover from what had already become a pretty extreme aircraft attitude. The injection of adrenaline from that incident was enough to keep us well focused for the rest of the journey!

M Flt Gazelles on Sir Percival's flight deck

At last we got to Southampton and landed, in turn, on the tiny flight deck of Sir Percival, each aircraft being folded before the next could land. As last to embark, I touched down on deck in mid to late afternoon, as I recall – some four to five hours after we had been due. As I stepped stiffly from the cockpit, the ships broadcast barked: 'FLIGHT COMMANDER TO THE BRIDGE!'. Unsuspectingly, I made my way to the bridge to be confronted by the ship's Captain – Tony Pitt – who berated me for being late and told me that I should be clear that he hated helicopters. In his experience helicopters and ships' routines just did not mix; having them on board was bad news and our late arrival, which had delayed his sailing, amply demonstrated this fact. I was to be clear that things would be run for the benefit of the ship and that M Flight would just have to work around that as best we could! I was about to point out that although the weather in Southampton was sunny and clear, there had been fog in Arbroath that morning and our delayed departure could not be helped. Fortunately, I had second thoughts and merely said 'Aye, Aye Sir', saluted, and left, thinking what bloody fun this is going to be for however long we end up embarked. I learned later of the immense pressures that Tony had been under, to turn his ship round from an intended refit and prepare for a voyage into the unknown, as well as the same family issues we all faced, and that my quick acceptance of his authority relieved at least one of his concerns. As it transpired, I have never worked with a ship's captain, RN or RFA, who did more to try and help an embarked flight but, at that moment, I was thinking how to make the best of what seemed an unpromising situation and that it was clear much work would be needed to establish a fruitful working relationship.

Even as the ship was about to sail, we were busily completing the Flight's preparations, as well as trying to dash off final letters to loved ones. Will Scott did not need to write:

I was ordered to the ships Wardroom to meet two visitors, who turned out to be my wife and mother - they had driven from Devon to say goodbye. They had stood at the gates of the military port at Marchwood for several hours insisting they weren't leaving until they were let on board! The gate guard relented when my wife told him she would cry if he didn't let them in."

We were still waiting for vital spare parts for the aircraft but were told they were shortly being delivered to a nearby naval shore establishment. So, with Sir Percival due to sail, I sent Bill O'Brien, with 'JC' Woods to a to collect them, hopefully to return before the ship departed. Unfortunately, the spare parts had not arrived and Sir Percival set sail into Southampton water in the gathering gloom. As Angus recalls:

Shortly after embarkation Sir Percival sailed, having delayed until we arrived, and proceeded in the fading light down Southampton Water. Having stowed our kit in our mess deck we went up to the weather deck to catch a last look at England. Whereas the main Task Force had set sail in a welter of flag waving euphoria televised on all the TV channels we slipped quietly out with just a little old lady on the Southampton side who was walking her small dog waving a white handkerchief at us to see us off.

It was dusk by the time the spare parts were delivered. With some qualms, I instructed Bill, who was not yet officially qualified for deck landings and armed only with the ships Plot of Intended Movement (PIM)[10], to rejoin us in Lime Bay, where the Captain was intending to spend the night settling down the ships company and newly embarked forces, and conducting emergency drills; I could not afford to disrupt the ships program for a second time on day one! Between them, Bill and JC did the job.

The next morning, before we left Lime Bay, Angus Horswill flew to Lee on Solent airfield to pick up more urgent equipment:

On arrival this so-called urgent kit turned out to be a pair of shotguns with ammunition and boxes of clay pigeons. What possible use these could be against our potential foes was beyond me, but I was just glad to go flying and to get another deck landing under my belt.

And so, thoroughly equipped for our journey, we headed out into the Atlantic Ocean

---

[10] QHI is a qualification required to teach pilots to fly. Every Squadron has one officially appointed to facilitate and oversee the maintenance of necessary flying qualifications – which includes a Squadron Acceptance check

Bill O'Brien conducting deck landing practice with Dolly Drummond

All at Sea: The Passage to Ascension Island

I had been proved wrong, we were not on leave but at sea and heading south towards the Falkland Islands. However, together with most of the Flight, I was still convinced that diplomacy would in the end prevail. The next 15 days at sea, were spent largely in an information vacuum. The Squadron HQ was on HMS Fearless, which had pressed ahead to link up with the Task Force Commander and the carrier group, leaving the slower RFA's, escorted by HMS Antelope, to make the best speed they could.

With no secure communications on board, we received little information, other than copies of the few signals that were distributed by our escort ship and the BBC World Service. Whilst deciding what to load, we had been told to assume that we would be operating from shipping, to reduce the amount of field equipment required, (such as Carlie Walker's cherished, customised, 4 ton based LAD workshop). So, in the absence of any other direction, we set about enhancing our ability to conduct flying operations from Sir Percival. The first few days were spent settling in, building relationships and protocols with the ship's officers and crew, whilst finding spaces from which to operate. John Hopkinson made it his business to befriend the ship's Sergeant Major and Flight Deck Officer (FDO) - a piratical looking Warrant Officer, from the Royal Corps of Transport's Maritime Regiment, called Neville Goodwin. John managed to persuade Goodwin to give us the use of a small cabin that was normally the flight deck store, to be used as our flight 'line office', from which aircraft maintenance was managed. Meanwhile, I applied my attention to the First Officer, Commander Peter Hill, who ran the ships programme, to secure enough flying serials to work up our deck operating skills. Deck landing training by day and night was the imperative since most of the Flight had never before operated from a ship.

Early on, we decided that it would be good to establish 'combat crews' both to balance experience and to develop better integration between pilots and observers. I was with Sandy Hamilton, whilst Will Scott teamed with Ken Priest, Bill O'Brien with Dolly Drummond and Angus Horswill with Bob Davenport. Terry Waldron, straight from pilot training, was paired with JC, our most experienced observer.

We began deck landing practice (DLP) as soon as possible but 9th April must have confirmed for Tony Pitt his worst suspicions about helicopters. Terry Waldron was flying his first sortie from a deck, with me supervising. Just after take-off, I noticed that he had forgotten to activate the emergency flotation gear. I do not remember which of us operated the switch but do remember the bang of two flotation bags rapidly inflating.

Get out of that!

The aircraft pitched violently nose down and I quickly grabbed the controls but nevertheless, we were alarmingly close to the water by the time everything was back under control. We then had to initiate an emergency recovery procedure, at great inconvenience to the ship. Having safely landed, we discovered that, with the floats inflated it was not possible to open the cabin doors. We were about to puncture the bags in our desire to get out, when John Hopkinson announced there were no spares and told us to wait for the LAD to remove the doors and lift them clear. We got a lot of stick from the rest of the flight, who claimed that we must have hit the wrong switch, but it transpired that the saline switches, designed as an automatic failsafe to activate the airbags, had become salt contaminated. To avoid repetition, all were disconnected!

Despite this setback, the ship was generous in its allocation of time for flying training serials and by the 15th of April, all pilots were current in day and night deck operations; we had even managed to prepare the observers to land on deck in the event of the pilot becoming disabled. Bill O'Brien didn't like the sound of pilots being disabled but noted that his observer, Dolly Drummond, "had a fair pair of hands so there was solace in that".

It had quickly become clear that a critical limitation on flying activity was a shortage of aviation trained staff in the ship', with a complement of only two helicopter controllers (HC) – Rob Gardiner and Phil Hanton, and one Flight Deck Officer (FDO), Neville Goodwin – all dual hatted from their primary tasks. To alleviate at least one element of the problem that was in our gift, Tony Pitt agreed that our Flight Sergeant, Ian Mellor, could be trained as a second FDO.

Sadly, Ian "crossed the bar" before I started writing this account, so cannot tell his own story but we all closely followed his progress. The first time he appeared on deck in his potential new role, he was wearing the whitest overalls we had ever seen, clearly straight out of stores and looking somewhat incongruous on a 'bootneck' Sergeant. We never witnessed what went on in 'ground school' but watched his practical training, at first with some amusement, as Neville Goodwin guided him through the marshalling signals, flapping Ian's arms for him, making him look more like a large flightless bird than an FDO. Somebody unkindly remarked "you'll never get airborne like that Ian!" But he made the grade and thereafter played a key role on the flight deck until we disembarked. He was rightly proud of his 'adqual'[11], feeling that he was contributing far more to the daily task than was, at this stage, allowed by his main, administrative role as the Flight SNCO.

It soon became clear that the Flight could contribute to the daily tasks of both Sir Percival and the wider Task Group. With only one larger Support Helicopter (SH) – based on RFA Stromness – in the Group, 'Teeny Weeny Airways (TWA)' as we were called (affectionately, we liked to think) were drawn into moving people, mail and stores between ships on a daily helicopter delivery service (HDS). This was a critical requirement when electronic signal connectivity was almost non-existent, and the only secure communication equipment was on HMS Antelope. Also, we were able to assist Sir Percival and other ships to work up their HCs, whilst maintaining our own competence in instrument flying skills and adding to our repertoire with radar Ship-Controlled Approaches (SCAs) and Extreme Low Visibility Approaches (ELVAs) - a convoluted but effective way of recovering onboard when the weather is really bad, which often it was. The detail is well described by Angus Horswill:

At this time the Gazelle AH1 had no electronic navigation aids whatsoever and was equipped with a very basic set of aircraft instruments. On top of that, although it had a basic stability augmentation system, the aircraft [like all helicopters] was basically unstable. The ship had a rudimentary radar and aircraft recovery procedure, but it was better than nothing if you went inadvertent [Instrument Meteorological Conditions] IMC and had to get back to the ship. At sea, hundreds of miles from the nearest land, there was nowhere else to go except swimming. The procedure was that as the ship steered into wind the HC gave you intercept headings to position you to approach the ship from the stern with a decent rate to approximate a 3-degree glidepath. If the visibility was so poor that you couldn't see the ship as you passed a height that should allow you to see the deck and land or carry out a missed approach without hitting the ship, then floating sodium flares would be thrown over the stern so that you could follow them at low speed and height to eventually find the ship and land on. The ability to be able to keep the aircraft under control at low level without any external references using instruments only was an essential skill in such a situation. This skill was also perishable, and it was vital to keep current.

---

[11] The term 'Adqual' is short for additional qualification, used in the RM to describe formal qualifications that do not fit into the main structure of branch qualifications.

Ten days into our odyssey Sir Percival awarded us the unofficial title of 'Sir Percy Flight'. I was content that our reputation was established!

Life on board gradually settled into routines. For some, seasickness was a constant presence. A flat-bottomed LSL in the Atlantic does not make for an entirely comfortable voyage. Some people fared much worse than others, whilst some did not feel it at all. After a while, it became less uncomfortable, but feelings of nausea still lingered. For the aircrew, there was some respite whilst flying but, after the relief of lifting clear of the heaving deck, it always felt much worse again after landing back on deck and waiting to be lashed down, with the tight neck seal of an immersion suit adding to the realization that they were not entirely free of seasickness quite yet. Another discomfort was a shortage of fresh water. Sir Percival's evaporator only made around four tonnes of freshwater a day, which was not enough for a fully loaded ship without external resupply. Showers became rationed; no more than one shower every other day and the water was only turned on for one hour. Strict instructions were issued to only dampen yourself, turn the water off, soap up and then rinse. For Will Scott it was a race against time:

You only once had to soap up and then find the water turned off when you tried rinse off, to know you should not risk that again. Walking around, covered in soap suds, with a towel around your waist, whilst trying to find a way of rinsing the shampoo from your hair without water was an experience not to be repeated!

For Monster the issue was about which meal you got to eat. He remembers:

The transit to Ascension Island was about the bad weather in the Bay of Biscay. The LAD and attached ranks who hadn't done any sea time, suffering with sea sickness and the antics in the galley with metal trays sliding around - main course, soup and desert all ending up in the one compartment of the tray. Depending on which end of the table you were sat at, you either ended up with your tray on the floor and your neighbours' tray or no tray at all!

In the absence of anything else, the world service had become our main source of 'strategic intelligence'. The emphasis was still on a 'diplomatic' solution, with the US Secretary of State, Al Haig, conducting 'shuttle diplomacy' between London and Buenos Aeries, followed by a Peruvian initiative, sometimes known as 'Haig Two'. At this stage of the adventure, we all still assumed that sooner or later, there would be a diplomatic solution and the mood remained relaxed. So, with time on our hands and the prospect of a prolonged trip with little by way of diversion, it was not long before mischief began!

We decided a good 'bite' was needed. This a traditional Naval Service pastime on long voyages, in which inexperienced sailors and marines are persuaded to undertake a task that any experienced hand would instantly recognise to be preposterous; the most apocryphally famous being to get volunteers to be the coxswain of a gunnery splash target[12]. A successful 'bite' depends on detailed fabrication and credibility. This 'bite' was

---

[12] A 'splash target' is used whilst doing joint gunnery firings with other ships or aircraft. The splash target is towed behind a non-firing ship at some distance to provide a target for others to aim at.

initiated with a 'spoof' signal, supposedly from Fleet HQ, planted in the signal log, which outlined a requirement for volunteers for 'special duties'. Our co-conspirator, Hugh McManners, a naval gunfire support officer (NGFSO) from 148 Meiktila Battery Royal Artillery, lent quasi-special forces (SF) credibility. The plot was simple. With SF stretched everywhere, each LSL was required to select and train its own team to be inserted ashore at night, in advance, to provide terminal guidance for the ships to beach and unload. The insertion was to be achieved using each LSL's own aircraft, which, in order not to compromise operational security, would have to maintain a steady course, at least half a kilometre off the coast, at a speed of 60 knots and altitude of 50 feet, whilst the shore party dropped into the water and swam ashore. It was called 'Helo-casting'. Within 24 hrs there were enough volunteers to warrant a 'selection process' and the 'bite' was on. The selection and training, overseen by Hugh McManners, became more outrageous as the days passed. The volunteers hung from the ships cranes in full assault order, to develop the muscle strength required to hang from the aircraft skids during the approach, practiced shark evasion drills, taped their ears to their heads in the style of rugby forwards, so they would not be damaged by the plunge into the water at 60 knots from 50 feet and much more besides. Whatever was asked of them they cheerfully did.

Their final pass-out exercise, supposedly to include a live drop, was conducted blindfold to simulate night operations. They crammed into the aircraft, which began its start up on the Flight Deck, while a crowd of onlookers quietly gathered to watch the denouement. At the critical moment, engines were cut blindfolds removed and there was

Helocasting rehearsal

the Captain, Tony Pitt, to present them with their 'Helocasting' wings, which comprised of a pair of weightlifter's arms either side of a sweating skull. Sadly, their commitment and courage went otherwise unrewarded!

More commonly known entertainments, such as a Line Crossing ceremony and ship's concert also helped to while away the time. In the former, King Neptune and his entourage were played by the older members of the ships company and embarked force, whilst those of us who were uninitiated became subject to Neptune's punishments for intruding into his kingdom, most of which involved getting covered by or immersed in various liquids, or being propositioned by a suspiciously hairy 'Mermaid'. At the concert, the Flight's sergeants gave a spirited rendition of 'Those Magnificent Men in Their Flying Machines', which probably confirmed everybody's deeply held views of us!

As we approached Ascension Island, we were content that, in terms of ships operations at least, we were as competent as we could be but we still had no idea of what was planned for us in the unlikely event that we did go to war, and time was starting to drag.

Those Magnificent Men...

Much Ado: Ascension Island and Preparation for War

After more than two weeks at sea, the period of uncertainty was coming to an end, as we approached Ascension Island for our rendezvous with the rest of the Task Force. On Tuesday 20th April, the Flight was tasked to fly ahead of the Antelope Task Group with despatches for HMS Fearless. I opted to fly the sortie with Bob Davenport and, whilst delivering the despatches, managed to snatch a hurried conversation on the flight deck with Andrew Eames, seeking to get some idea of what was going on. Andrew told me that the Amphibious Group would be assembling at Ascension Island and that we would all be disembarking to allow the ships to be restowed in a configuration more appropriate for an amphibious landing and the aircraft to be modified. He suggested that we flew on to land at Ascension Island's 'Wideawake' airfield, to await the arrival of the shipping. At the time, Wideawake airfield was run by the United States Air Force (USAF). The reason for this was three-fold, firstly to support a CIA listening post, second Ascension was at the end of the Cape Canaveral military missile range and thirdly the island had one of the transmitters for the Very Low Frequency Omega system that was used for navigation and communication by submerged nuclear submarines. For all of

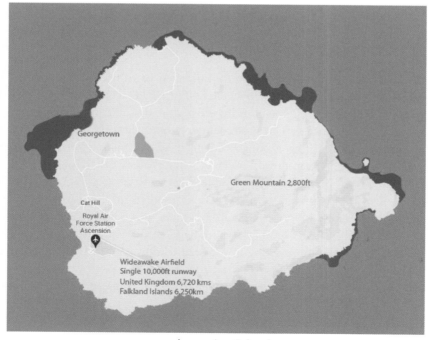

Ascension Island

25

that, Wideawake initially proved to be anything but that; there was no response from the control tower to our requests for clearance to land and the airfield appeared to be deserted so, in the end, we just did it and then waited for somebody to contact us.

Eventually, a USAF master sergeant turned up to enquire what we were doing there; it seemed that we were not the only ones who had been in an information vacuum. However, within hours the place was transformed, as ships began to disembark their aircraft, clearing deck space for the forthcoming 'restow', and the first elements of the air bridge from the UK began to arrive.

Physically linking up with the Squadron HQ for the first time since this venture had begun, and after being out of communication since we had embarked, we learned that much had been happening, both before departure and during the time we had been at sea. On the 17th April, the Task Force commanders had met with C-in-C Fleet, Admiral Sir John Fieldhouse, and a campaign plan had been agreed. On the 20th, with no sign of compromise from the Argentine Government, the British War Cabinet had ordered the Task Force to repossess the islands. Suddenly, things became less relaxed and we were gripped by a new sense of urgency, though still with the thought that the situation would eventually be resolved by diplomacy before any shooting started.

New equipment had been ordered and began to arrive. Our Gazelle helicopters were to be fitted with with two rocket pods, each pod carrying six French, 68mm 'Matra' free flight rockets as well as infra-red (IR) exhaust diffusers, and there were technical modifications to allow a substantial increase of "maximum all up mass[13]" from 1800kg to 2100kg. Still to be delivered were first generation passive night goggles (PNG), a relatively new technology that had been bought from the USA. All of this required substantial modifications to the aircraft but, undaunted, our small LAD rolled up their sleeves and set to work enthusiastically.

In addition, our CO, Peter Cameron, directed us to use our own ingenuity to locally produce a mount that would allow general-purpose machine guns (GPMG) to be fired from the Gazelles, since no such thing existed in any inventory, anywhere. There was disagreement between the flight commanders about the optimum solution. Some favoured a fixed forward firing mount, controlled by the pilot others, including me, argued that the forward arc was already covered by the rockets and that, despite the extra weight, a manned waist mount would provide flank protection and greater flexibility. Unable to resolve the disagreement, Peter left us each to go our own way, the only proviso being that, before any mount could be flown, it would have to be cleared by Larry Rotchell, a young REME Captain in command of the Squadron's LAD. With the volume of untried modifications being introduced to our aircraft, I thought Larry was bearing a level of responsibility way beyond that which should reasonably have been expected of him and was surprised that more senior REME representation had not been

---

[13] All up mass is the total weight to which an aircraft is cleared to operate and includes the airframe itself together with fuel, crew and any passengers or supplies being carried.

flown forward to take on that burden. However, Larry was lucky to be supported by an exceptionally talented and experienced ASM, Barry Marshall.

Whilst the LAD laboured on the aircraft, the aircrew had new skills to learn. With no experience of rocket firing or night vision devices, there was a lot of talk and making it up as we went along! The rockets had arrived almost immediately and after a couple of days frenetic activity on the part of the LAD, the first aircraft were ready, and firings were set to occur.

The sighting system for the rockets was, at best, rudimentary. It comprised a pointed plastic rod mounted on the Aerial Direction Finding (ADF) antenna. The calibration was achieved by the LAD aligning a mathematically calculated point on the rear cockpit bulkhead and the pointed tip of the rod to an aiming point on which each rocket pod was bore sighted. Finally, each pilot sat in the cockpit and indicated where on the cockpit canopy their line of sight to the aiming point matched that of the calculated line and a marker pen was used to make a cross at that point - a different colour for each pilot because of their differing seat position and head height. The theory was that, with the aircraft in balance and the cross aligned with the top of the candle, the rockets could be expected go in roughly the right direction.

An understandably hesitant USAF Base Commander had been persuaded to allocate an area to use as a range for our first firings on Friday 23rd April. Space was scarce on the Island and our range consisted of a rocky promontory, south west of the

White 'Candle' sight on ADF Antenna

27

Firing a "Ripple 12"

airfield, with its fuel farm to one side and a bird sanctuary to the other. The target was a pile of oil drums in the centre of the range. There was a degree of tension building since, as far as we were aware, there had been no previous testing on a Gazelle of the rocket system, which was designed normally to be fitted to fixed wing aircraft. When the Squadron HQ had asked for expert advice on fitting and firing the rockets, they received the reply "when you have fitted and fired them you will be the experts"! Peter Cameron, had bravely elected to fly the first, 'proving' sortie, so the rest of us, together with the Base Commander, were huddled in an observation post overlooking the range, to see how it went. A full load comprised 12 rockets which, depending how you set up the switches, could be fired singly, in pairs, ripples of 6 rockets or the whole lot at once. Peter positioned his Gazelle in a high hover at the allocated firing point, with the intention of firing a couple of single rockets, followed by a couple of pairs with the final serial being a 'ripple' shot of the remaining ordnance whilst in forward flight. With tension palpable, the countdown began and, as it reached zero, Peter's Gazelle disappeared in a cloud of smoke and was literally pushed backwards. He had inadvertently fired all 12 rockets at once and they all landed in the bird sanctuary. The Base Commander was ashen white and going into either shock or apoplexy, so Andrew Eames attempted to calm him, "Cheer up it could have been worse, it could have been the fuel farm"! Inconsolable, the Base Commander declared the range closed and stormed off, leaving us to wonder how we could master this weapon system with no range on which to practice firing it.

However, later that day, the range was reopened, and, over the next few days, we all got to fire, with varying degrees of success and no further avian casualties. The fuel farm also remained unscathed! I have since learned that Peter Cameron had gone to the Base Commander to persuade him to permit us to continue with this vital training and explain "it was only finger problems on my part that caused the accidental discharge and I was sorry to disturb his birds. I think yet another bottle of Scotch effectively pacified him!"

Over the next few days, we continued training with the rockets, each firing around 12 rounds to become qualified to operate the system. How standards were set is anybody's guess because none of us, including the assessors, had done anything like this before.

Loading the rockets proved equally challenging for the LAD. Charlie Walker recalled that the instructions for arming the rockets and loading them into the pods were all in French.

To arm individual rockets there was a small plastic pin which had to be inserted a certain way and a part then broken off (all done by trial and error as none of us could read French). It was not until we

Ian Stewart and Charlie Walker loading Matra rockets at Wideawake

had done a couple that we realized we were sat upon the crates containing all the supply of rockets. Could have been a big bang if we had got it wrong!"

John Hopkinson was superb in managing the large and complex engineering requirement placed on his small team and, not for the last time on this trip, I realised how lucky we were to have a man of his ability to support us. He had spent time on the first part of our voyage, building a good relationship with the Chief Engineer of Sir Percival, Captain Alan Johnson, which he now put to good use, working with the ship's engineers deep in the bowels of the ship, to manufacture the components for the machine gun mounts that he had personally designed. The challenges in both design and manufacture were to ensure sufficient robustness against the recoil of a medium machine gun firing long bursts, having an effective means of containing spent clips and cartridges (so that we did not end up with one or more of them being sucked into our one and only engine) and to limit traverse, to prevent us shooting bits off our own aircraft! Having been fitted and fine-tuned by Charlie Walker and Ian Stewart, the prototype worked perfectly and was passed fit for service, allowing production of two further mounts to continue. However, we were back at sea before they were ready for training.

Whilst we were delighted to have gained some armament, there were drawbacks and compromises to be made. First, there was a weight penalty, especially regarding the GPMG, which used much of the additional power that we had gained. Also, the rocket pods were not compatible with the Gazelle flotation gear; whilst this would not matter much, once ashore, flotation was not something that we really wanted to be without in the middle of the South Atlantic.

There, was also a debate about the body armour that we had been issued. Armoured seats had been ruled out, due to all the other weight being added and the difficulty of getting out of them if forced to ditch in the sea, but we were issued the chest plates that normally form part of the whole. We were not sure how effective the plates would be without the rest of the seat and wondered, if we had to ditch in the sea with no flotation gear fitted, did we really want that extra weight strapped to us? The solution, as I recall, was to place the plate under the seat cushion, so at least one precious part was protected!

Most of the Brigade had by now disembarked and just about everything was landed, repacked and reloaded to conform to the landing plan that had now been developed. At the same time, the Commando and Para units were taking the opportunity to stretch their legs and carry out some military training on dry land, whilst the logistic build up from the UK grew by the hour; Wideawake was by now living up to its name!

Until now there had been only a trickle of personal mail being collected by SH when we were close enough to land. Now the floodgates opened with letters flowing in both directions. Alyson Priest had heard nothing since Ken sailed,

but at last I received the longest letter I'd ever had from Ken! It had been a long wait for any news but of course there was no means of getting mail away from the ships until the arrival at Ascension Island.

Not only was there a backlog of mail from families and girlfriends but also sack loads of pen friend letters from young ladies who the Sun, or one of the other Red Tops, had exhorted to support the lads. The pen-pal letters were shared out, for sailors and marines to answer.

The Squadron operated around a small hangar on the Airfield that served as workshop and transit centre for the rapidly increasing flow of materiel arriving from the UK. The technicians were constantly busy but, between flying training serials, the aircrew had little to do except to conduct ground or air tests, as required by the LAD and that only needed a couple of crews to be available. Those required for duty or to continue work on the aircraft, slept on the floor at the side of the hangar; the remainder were flown back to Sir Percival in the evening, to live more comfortably, then moved ashore again in the morning. It was difficult to sleep at the airfield, where activity often ran through the night. I recall, one occasion being rudely awakened by a couple of newly arrived RAF transport pilots demanding to know where the 'aircrew' accommodation was. Their faces were a picture when I waved my arm around the array of sleeping bags huddled along the walls of the small hangar and said, "we are the aircrew, this is it!"

But even the relative comfort of Sir Percival was limited. As JC recalled:

When we returned in the evening, the water would be switched on, to give us the chance to have a shower and dhobi. The food was adequate, the beer warm, showers limited and, with the ship in overload conditions, there was limited if any air conditioning.

However, there was other respite to be found for those who could contrive to slip away. The easiest bolthole, for those in the know, was the Cable and Wireless Club in Georgetown, the Island's capital, where it was possible to chill over a beer and a sandwich. Will Scott hooked up with an old 'batch mate[14]' and fellow helicopter pilot, Ron Crawford (also ashore on Ascension with 846 Sqn) and with Pete Reynolds, leader of 846 Sqn's Mobile Air Operations Team (MAOT). Purloining the MAOT team Land Rover, the three set off to the summit of Green Mountain, where there is an abandoned barracks that, in previous times had housed the Island's Royal Marines Garrison. There they found a tunnel dug through the mountain by those Royal Marines. Intrigued they decided to explore it:

Holding on to each other (nose to tail like elephants) we crept through the tunnel in the dark and were delighted to emerge at a pub called The Red Lion. It was Sunday lunch time, so a pint at The Red Lion seemed appropriate… who would've thought!

For the more adventurous, there was the lure of the SS Canberra, a large white cruise ship that had been pressed into service as a troop ship, with a makeshift flight deck fitted where its swimming pool used to be. With the help of friends in 45 Commando, who were embarked on Canberra, JC Woods managed to spirit himself on board for 24 hours of undetected, informal R&R, in the comparative luxury that she afforded.

---

[14] Intakes of Royal Marines officers going through basic training are known as Young Officer Batches.

One evening the Canberra's liberty boat appeared carrying out cross decking operations. I decided, as we were going to war, there was nothing to lose, so I ran to the mess deck, grabbed my ID card and cheque book and jumped on to the liberty boat, shouting back to Bill and Ken "cover for me, I'll be back in the morning". Arriving on Canberra was a different world, room to move and air conditioning, I went straight to the Sergeants Mess bar and ordered a pint of lager, "Sorry ran out yesterday", so was forced to have a cold bottled beer dripping with condensation, what a way to go to war! I met up with a few 'oppos'[15], found a spare bed and a dhobi machine, stripped naked and chucked everything into the dhobi machine, borrowed a track suit and got pleasantly pissed while my dhobi was washed. I even found an iron to ensure I still looked smart when I returned to the Percival. The next morning, again a different world, with kippers for breakfast; Canberra had sailed fully loaded with food for a civilian cruise. I returned to Sir Percival at lunchtime the next day and was advised I had the "runs" if anyone asked. What a swift R&R it was but improved my morale!

Seeking to emulate this good fortune, Bill O'Brien and Dolly Drummond were not so lucky.

Dolly and I 'blagged' a ride on an LCM[16] and escaped to Canberra, where I still had lots of mates in 42, with the intention of sampling the fine wine and dining experience overnight. We were just sitting down in the first-class restaurant when, 'Sgt O'Brien, your Flight Commander requires your immediate return to RFA Sir Percival!' was piped. Busted, never got a drink or a bite!

Even Sir Percival's Captain Tony Pitt started to look for diversions. Knowing his love of the game I had told him there was a golf course on the Island. Now aware of our capacity to set up a bite, I think he was suspicious, but the potential opportunity was too great and he asked me to fly him out to have a look at it before he challenged his brother, Captain of another of the RFAs, to a game. Having satisfied himself that there really was a course Tony asked me to fly past his brother's ship so that a challenge could be issued:

That was a ride I'll never forget. Considering my stated dislike of helicopters, I must have had a lot of faith in you! I remember waving my putter in the direction of my brother at the time and I think he realised my thoughts. On the way home I did play the course with other members of the ship's company similarly inclined but my bro was not with us.

However, the Flight's groundcrew did not enjoy the same freedoms. Monster, "never did put my feet on dry land until we landed in San Carlos Water". But life on board Sir Percival did have its own distractions:

At Ascension I spent a lot of time on the rear of the ship, with the Chinese crew, fishing. Having built up a good relationship with them, I would get an invite to their quarters for a drink (No Canberra for us!). This was an experience. I went to the heads

[15] Oppo: Special friend or chum in a ship or unit… (Jolly 1999 p314)
[16] Landing Craft Mechanised are– designed primarily for moving vehicles ashore

only to discover they had isolated the smoke detector and had turned a shower cubicle into a smoke room, the fish we had been catching were hanging in there.

On Monday 26th April, an alarm was raised. An Argentinean freighter had been seen in a Spanish port and a scare sprang up that Argentinean SF had somehow used it to spirit themselves onto the island, with the intention to gather intelligence and conduct sabotage. The ships of the Amphibious Task Group implemented a standard procedure called 'Operation Awkward', which involves weather deck sentries dropping grenades with 7 sec fuses overboard at regular intervals to deter combat swimmers. I have no idea how successful this is against combat swimmers, but it certainly deterred those sleeping on board from a good night's sleep. Each time a charge went off, the entire ship rang and shuddered until, finally one sleep deprived Colour Sergeant, in no uncertain terms, told the sentry who was responsible for this, that 'if he threw one more explosive charge into the water he'd be going over the side with it'.

In retrospect it all seems a little farcical; it even seemed a bit far-fetched at the time, but it kept us all exercised. Will Scott and Dolly Drummond, together with the Squadron Commander, flew a low-level sortie all around the coast of Ascension, looking for signs of a rubber dinghy or frogmen. Neither were found but several sea birds died as they had never seen a helicopter before and simply flew about periodically being hit by rotor blades. Meanwhile, I spent the day on ground alert, ready to provide fire support to ground operations with our shiny new rockets!

Routine liaison tasking was also going on. Angus Horswill was tasked to fly to a tented camp on the northern side of the island and drop a high-ranking officer:

Having found it, I circled several times to find a suitable landing spot. Eventually, having selected a spot, I endeavoured to do a low powered zero speed landing to minimise any recirculation of volcanic dust but, despite my best effort, I still managed to stir up a substantial cloud that slowly drifted over some of the camp. Once shut down my passenger scuttled off whilst I stayed with the aircraft. Whilst sitting in the aircraft minding my own business, I spied a naval officer resplendent in best tropical whites, complete with magnificent voluminous shorts, stomping towards me from the direction of the camp that I had just treated to a light dusting. Recognising trouble approaching I decided that the only way to head this off was with maximum bullshit. I came smartly to attention as best I could in flying gear and gave him a salute that did the Household Brigade proud. He then attempted to dress me down quoting someone called FONAC [Flag Officer Naval Air Command] who had banned naval helicopters landing anywhere on Ascension other than the airfield. I pointed out to him that I was an Army Pilot and that I hadn't a clue who FONAC was (I did really). Failing to notice the large words Royal Marines painted down the side of the aircraft and somewhat taken aback he told me basically that I was a very naughty pilot, not to do it again and beat a hasty retreat.

The sabotage scares continued, with M Flight supporting cordon and search operations by 45 Commando, as the entire landing force scoured the island in search of the shadowy Argentinean SF. It must have been hard work for the marines on the ground but for us aviators, it provided a welcome break from the dust and noise of the airfield and an opportunity to practice terrain flying, as opposed to operating solely over the flat

First generation PNG

expanses of the Atlantic Ocean. On one occasion 45 Commando planned a pre-dawn sweep of the Green Mountain. We were tasked to support them with 'nightsun'[17], to provide illumination. This obliged our LAD to labour through the night to remove the newly fitted rockets from one aircraft, in order to fit the nightsun equipment, only to reverse the process on completion of the operation.

As the sabotage alarm started to give way to reason and with departure from Ascension Island imminent, we turned our attention to the next new skill that we needed to acquire – flying with PNG. These were first generation night vision devices, full face goggles with bifocal lenses and quite heavy, which unbalanced flying helmets and strained the wearers neck. The Squadron Commander's directive was that each flight should aim to have one 'PNG capable' crew available by the time that we arrived at the Falkland Islands, but I cannot recall any particular guidance about how we were to achieve this.

My own arrogance, supported by the fact that, after Angus Horswill, I had the most pilot hours in the Flight, axiomatically made me one half of the PNG crew, the only decision was who would fly with me; it was not difficult. Back in Scotland, I had seen clearly that Bill O'Brien was the most naturally competent pilot in the flight, and it was his skills I wanted with me for this step into the unknown. At this stage, we still did not have the real PNG but the daylight simulators had arrived, so we took the opportunity to conduct a little 'overland' simulation training, reckoning that the next time we would fly over land would probably be on operations in the Falkland Islands. The daylight simulators had no image intensification capability and were optically neutral with green filters to simulate the night view. They made the world look remarkably like the world, only green. Even so, it was not easy. These first-generation goggles were bulky, heavy and allowed no peripheral visual cueing. This necessitated, much more head movement to maintain spatial awareness and all normal sense of perspective was lost in the green monotone with which PNG portrayed the world. We each flew a sortie wearing the daylight simulator, with the other as safety pilot, it was not a pleasant experience and we soon realised the challenge that lay ahead. To the uninitiated, being offered equipment that allows you to 'see in the dark' may seem to be a bonus, but it required us to develop a whole new way of flying. To appreciate the difficulty, you would need to drive your car through a city centre, looking only through two toilet rolls with green cling film stretched over the end!

Bill O'Brien describes our first training session:

Lesson One of 'Teach Yourself How to Fly on Goggles' (TYHFG) passed largely without incident, giving us some confidence to try the real thing. Downstream they proved better than flying unaided, a bit like cotton buds to get into those awkward little places, but were clearly much less capable than later iterations, particularly in low light conditions, which was the case most of the time.

---

[17] Effectively a searchlight strapped to the side of the helicopter; developed for use in Northern Ireland to provide more durable illumination for ground troops to operate.

Unfortunately, we had no time to do more before we were back at sea.

Game On: Heading to War

Wednesday 28th April saw another turn of the ratchet on the road to war. As the Carrier Task Group neared the Falkland Islands, the previously established 'Exclusion Zone' was declared to be a 'Total Exclusion Zone', within which any Argentine ships or aircraft would be attacked without warning. A sense of anticipation was now starting to mount and, with news of the recapture of South Georgia by M Company of 42 Commando, morale was high. This news also carried the bonus that the sinking of the Argentinean submarine 'Santa Fe' during that operation, meant there was one less to worry about on our own journey south. Up until now, our campaign had been mostly a light-hearted adventure but, in the light of this news, there was a growing feeling that, if we left Ascension to go south, we would likely be 'going to war' and the only way we would be coming back was after that war was over, or not at all. A more sober atmosphere began to settle on the Flight. With efforts to broker peace continuing, I was still not wholly convinced that it would come to an amphibious assault on the Islands, but we needed to train and prepare as if it would. Like all other commanders, high and low, I am sure, I was determined to ensure that, in the given circumstances, we would be as proficient and prepared as was possible.

With the 're-stow' completed, the Brigade re-embarked and, on Thursday 29th April, the LSL element of Amphibious Task Group, set off on the next leg of its journey south. Although we didn't know it at the time, HMS Fearless (on which 3 BAS HQ was embarked) and HMS Intrepid[18], capable of faster transit speeds, remained at Ascension Island for another week to practice some of the pre-assault evolutions, in particular the removal of a known Argentinean OP on Fanning Head, which overlooked our chosen landing area. Most aircraft modifications had been completed but we still needed a lot of practice to become competent in using this new equipment, all of which now would have to happen at sea. Fortunately, in the early days of this second leg of our passage, we were afforded ample opportunity to fly, in order to develop the necessary skills.

Having failed to materialise before we sailed from Ascension Island, the real PNG finally arrived, parachuted to us at sea. So it was that, after a couple more 'simulator' sorties, Bill O'Brien and I conducted our first real PNG sortie from a tiny, pitching flight deck in the dark of a South Atlantic night! Even though we launched and recovered in a

---

[18]HMS Fearless and HMS Intrepid were the two Landing Platforms Dock (LPDs) in the task force and vital for their ability to support both helicopter and landing craft operations as well as provide command centres. The Combined Amphibious HQ was embarked on HMS Fearless, as was our own Squadron HQ.

conventional manner, with the assistance of deck lighting and a glide slope indicator, it was a harrowing experience. As Bill recalls it:

'TYHFG' Lesson 2: The first time at night and with us both on goggles began. We had no idea of what we were supposed to be seeing and no one to tell us, but we did agree that seeing not much of anything at all, except for a green haze, was probably the best we could expect. We had no way of assessing whether the light levels were suitable for flight and quite frankly, with the lack of ambient light and overcast, everything was just, well, the same shade of green. Getting the aircraft skids stuck in the netting around the flight deck gave us a few nervy minutes but we completed the sortie with the aircraft, if not our dignity, intact. We reflected that this was probably not an act of war, just then anyway.

Others had clearly been observing our progress and I was most grateful, on return, to find a large tot of whiskey awaiting me in the Wardroom, accompanied by a note saying, 'With the compliments of the Captain!'. Two days later, our nerves were sufficiently recovered to attempt a second sortie, which went much better, giving us the confidence that we might become fully proficient by the time we reached the Falkland Islands.

The PNG were not the only thing parachuted to us; we were also receiving occasional mail drops. Although he had never seen one of the original pen pal letters, Will Scott was surprised to receive a passionate letter from a female wrestler named Wilma, who had been thrilled by his amorous reply to her original missive and could not wait to get to grips with him! He never did find out for sure who had set him up but has his suspicions.

It was now over a month since we had left Arbroath, we were on the second leg of our passage to the Falkland Islands, having re-equipped and re-arranged ourselves on Ascension Island. Still without any secure communications on board, we continued to rely on the BBC World Service, which was relayed over the ship's broadcast system, to try and assess what might lie ahead. Its signature tune, 'Lillibulero', became the signal for an increasingly engaged audience to cluster round the speakers to hear the latest developments.

On Saturday 1st May, we heard that ships and aircraft from the Carrier Task Group had bombarded Stanley Airport and that the Argentineans had retaliated with Mirage jets attacking British ships. At this point, there were no serious losses and there seemed still to be a possibility that diplomacy would be the eventual solution. However, the following day, the Argentinean Cruiser, the 'General Belgrano' was sunk by HMS Conqueror, a nuclear-powered hunter killer submarine; 'Gotcha' said The Sun newspaper. Two days later, on 4th May, HMS Sheffield was put out of action by an Argentinean air launched Exocet missile; in both cases, but particularly the Belgrano, there were heavy casualties. With so much blood spilt, we now thought it certain that neither side would back down without a more serious fight, even though Peru was still trying to craft a peace plan.

The focus of our daytime training was learning to accurately fire the Matra rockets and waist mounted GPMGs, using a 'splash target' that was being towed by our new escort ship, HMS Antrim. Given our proficiency at that stage, it was probably the most dangerous evolution that HMS Antrim thought she would conduct during the entire campaign! Bill O'Brien was flying one such sortie:

The GPMG waist gun was quite successful, but we were still struggling with rocket technique. In the last serial a rocket actually flew over Antrim's Flight Deck and the HC angrily informed us that if we didn't return to Mother[19] [Sir Percival] immediately there would be no need for us to worry about the Argies because, in his own words, 'we'll f****** shoot you down ourselves'

To the annoyance of our observers, I suspect, I decided that we needed also to train some of our aircraft handlers to become GPMG 'door gunners', in order to provide the numbers required to sustain 'three crew' operations with three aircraft. There was stiff competition, but we eventually chose John MacKenzie, Martin Walkinshaw and Chris Roberts.

I do not have clear recollection of the chronology of next few weeks, as we relentlessly proceeded south, and my logbook does not really help arrange them, since flying opportunities were limited by weather, course and security restrictions. However, a few highlights remain vividly in my memory.

Sandy Hamilton manning the 'Hopkinson' GPMG waist mount

---

[19] Used by FAA as radio shorthand for the ship on which an aircraft is embarked.

Bill O'Brien and I managed another few, vital hours of PNG training, not as much as we had hoped but enough to sufficiently develop our confidence, despite having seriously scared ourselves when we decided to leave the immediate vicinity of Sir Percival ship's circuit, to 'buzz' HMS Antrim, our group escort. Whatever made us think that buzzing a warship at action stations, in a war zone, in the dark, with no warning was a good idea soon became irrelevant. Light levels dropped below minima and, although we now recognised the phenomena, we were stuck with it. The Task Group had now adopted strict electronic emission control measures, which meant we were operating in an environment that allowed no light or radio communication; to call for either risked compromising the security of the entire Group. After five to ten extremely uncomfortable minutes, we almost ran into the side of a ship which, thankfully, turned out to be Sir Percival, to which we recovered with elevated heart rates and feeling more than slightly foolish! Angus Horswill who, as duty pilot, had been watching us from the bridge wing, using an image intensifying weapon site, knew we had been in all kinds of trouble and was waiting for Bill in the POs & Sgts' Mess, almost as white faced as was Bill.

But, if night deck landings with PNG were scary, doing them without, in that environment, was arguably worse. Will Scott and I were practicing standard night circuits and, in accordance with procedure, the only light Sir Percival was showing was the dimmed horizon bar, necessary to achieve a conventional night deck landing. As we took off and cleared away from the flight deck, we could see nothing at all. Will remembers,

It was a dark, overcast night, with absolutely no visible horizon. We immediately switched to flying on instruments [not best done at 100 feet above sea level] and contrived to fly a 'box circuit' hoping and praying we would see the ship again. At 1,500 miles from land, with no way of contacting the ship and in pitch darkness it was a considerable relief when the dim horizon bar lights on Sir Percival's flight deck came into view. We didn't try that again!

With the prospect of combat near certain, we started, increasingly, to develop the discussion, started at Squadron level whilst at Ascension, on likely tasks and how best to conduct them. There was no relevant UK Army Aviation doctrine and very little of our previous tactical flying training seemed relevant, so we talked about adapting basic military tactics, techniques and procedures, such as 'fire and manoeuvre', to the aviation environment. The problem was that we could only talk; the first time we would be able to practice and test our thoughts, would be for real. It was during one of these discussions that Will Scott bravely spoke out, to ask what value small lightly armed and fragile helicopters could add to the work of the more robust support helicopters. With no other answer available, my 'off the cuff' response turned out to be chillingly prescient. I said that, if nothing else, light helicopters could check a route ahead of the support helicopters, because it was better to lose a Gazelle than a Sea King full of marines.

It was during this period that we received an instruction from Squadron HQ, detailing the procedure to be followed when firing Matra rockets at ground targets. We were never clear on the source of this instruction but, since Squadron HQ had no access to either aircraft or rockets, we presumed that some 'boffins' back in UK, divorced from the reality of war, had worked it out. The instruction set out that the optimum launch profile was to approach the target fast, at low level and at right angles to the intended launch direction; at an indeterminant optimum moment, we should start a rapid climb, both to gain height and identify the target, before rolling into an attacking dive and launching the rockets. We tried it and immediately became dubious about the chances of surviving long enough to launch rockets in the agonisingly long process of pulling up and rolling into an attacking dive, never mind extracting ourselves after launch. From our own experience of the inaccurate sighting system, we decided that firing rockets singly or in pairs and walking them onto a target was the most viable modus operandi. But more importantly, providing close air support from a Gazelle did not strike us as an act of war in any case; we had perceived the rockets to be something to use to get ourselves out of trouble, not into it, so we quietly ignored the instruction! Happily, as I later learned, the Squadron HQ team had reached a similar conclusion and had rejected the only request that was made for such a mission, during the closing battles around Stanley.

One evening, there was intelligence that a Soviet satellite had been reoriented to overfly the task force, whether simply for their own information or to pass some to Argentina was not clear. However somebody, it might even have been the Captain, suggested that an appropriate message should be sent. So, as the satellite passed overhead, as many of us as possible crowded onto the upper deck and collectively "mooned" towards the heavens!

There followed a couple of days of ferocious seas, as we passed through the 'roaring forties' which, even though we all now had our 'sea legs', were challenging. With a cabin close to the stern, I had to strap myself into my bunk bed at night, to avoid being tossed out of it. But the weather did not stop everything. It was the birthday of one of the ship's officers, and so a small party was thrown in the Wardroom to celebrate. The ship was pitching and rolling so violently that it was impossible to stand comfortably but, not about to miss out on a party, we sat splay legged in a circle and handed round the drinks being passed out from the wardroom bar by an equally sedentary purser.

Mealtimes often caused hilarity, the cooks were part of the RFA's Hong Kong Chinese crew, who steadfastly continued to serve such things as soup for starters in the wardroom. On a flat-bottomed boat rolling 20 degrees either side of the upright and pitching 20 or 30 feet up and down every 2 minutes, this was a truly masterful attempt to 'keep calm and carry on'. As Will Scott put it:

Who could forget the cauldron of soup, ingeniously strung to strong points in the galley, swinging magnificently over a stove ring, in a bid to keep it warm and stop it spilling, whilst the Chinese cooks strove to serve it in bowls? Of course, the second challenge was eating it, the Fleet Auxiliary use a clever, sticky rubber mat on dining tables; once a bowl was placed upon a mat it rarely moved, only the soup did.

When the sea calmed a little, we resumed necessary flying operations but with real fear for the safety of the LAD and ground handlers as they manhandled the aircraft around the heaving decks, more than once leading to somebody falling into the safety netting that surrounded the deck. There was real bravery being shown to get those aircraft ready to fly. In the understated words of Charlie Walker:

> To start with, the spreading of rotor blades and manhandling aircraft across the flight deck became hairy at times but, as with all things, it got better and less worrying the more it happened. The worst time I can remember was as we refitted the rotor blades, on approach to the Islands, in seas so big that the other ships disappeared behind the waves! But, by then, everybody knew the job inside out and we got it done.

Having linked together all elements of the Amphibious Task Group and joined with the Task Force Commander in the Carrier Group, final plans were made. On 19th May, the weather allowed final 'pre-D Day' cross decking to take place, to move the assault waves into appropriate but very overloaded and uncomfortable assault ships. We did a huge amount of communication flying that day. I recall vividly the majestic sight of the entire Task Force seen hazily from the air, with ships of every size, shape and description spread to the horizon in every direction. It seemed as if the entire British Fleet was concentrated in one single endeavour, which was not far from the truth.

As we got closer to our destination, a new threat was introduced, the possibility of being attacked by an Argentine submarine. To prepare for the worst and save our precious aircraft, if we could, we agreed on a drill that, if the ship called 'contact', the LAD and handlers would dash to the flight deck and prepare the first helicopter for flight, whilst the aircrew donned their immersion suits. The first practice was hilarious, the ground crew had no trouble, but the aircrew spent ages falling about on the floor struggling to get into their immersion suits in a combination of heavy swell and confined space, eventually arriving on deck black and blue with bruises. The routine was practiced once or twice more until the ships broadcast announced that there would be no more practices; the next alarm would be genuine. Whilst we were relieved to stop, it was an ominous moment of reality.

During the ship's preparations for the final approach, we were allocated a small space at the rear of the ships bridge to use as a CP, with radios that would connect to the 3BAS communication network and a duty pilot who also had direct access to the bridge watchkeepers. This setup subsequently became extremely useful during the first couple of days of the battle of San Carlos Water, as we were often able to give the bridge crew much earlier warning of air raids than they were receiving from the naval net, as well as an up to date land tactical situation which as greatly appreciated. We received also an unexpected bonus. The LAD was instructed to clear out the flight deck store, which they had been using as the Flight line office, in order for it to be available as a shelter for flight deck personnel, in the event of an air raid. In so doing, they came across a stash of prized Hawkins mountain boots, and arctic windproof smocks, which had no indicated recipient and had clearly been overlooked at some unknown point in the past. In time-honoured naval tradition, they were duly 'proffed[20]' and distributed within the flight.

The final approach necessitated a daylight transit, to arrive at the planned landing zone, San Carlos Water, at night. We all felt quite tense during this last stage of our passage. We were sure the Argentineans would know where we were but what would they do? We did not have air superiority, supposedly a doctrinal necessity for amphibious landings so, not only did the possibility of a raid seem high but also, they still had submarines at sea, which presented a dilemma, well summarised by Will Scott:

> If you were not at a duty station, the perceived safest place to be, was in the bowels of the ship. It was a very nervy feeling sitting in an enclosed steel box at water level, wondering which wall the torpedo was going to come through … Suffice to say that event never occurred. Alarms came from our escort ship, HMS Antelope, but were later presumed to be erroneous, possibly caused by whales.

Mercifully, it became foggy during the final approach, which reduced the air threat so, as Will recounts, "most of us opted for the open deck rather than the confines of the lower decks". We were all aware we were about to make history, conducting an amphibious assault against an established enemy force; none of us knew what our future would be. The tension was palpable and was exacerbated by having nothing to do. M Flt had been designated as the Squadron reserve for D Day and everything was as ready as it could be. We were now simply passengers, reliant on the skill and luck of our own ship's company and those of the escorting warships. The 45 Commando Chaplain, Wynn Jones, held a small service on the 'gun deck'. He was impressed by the turn out but keen to impress upon us that attendance did not absolve us from the possibility of meeting our maker!

On 13th May direction from London to adjust routine to suit conditions in the Falkland Islands, whilst remaining on GMT had led to time becoming almost meaningless in human terms. From that date we were obliged to live in 'Zulu time' (the universal time for UK military operations) but the 4-hour time difference to local time dislocated any relationship between clocks, darkness and light, in which a soldier's body clock favours the latter! As Tony Pitt's Post Operation Report records

> *Over the next few days, the routine on [Sir Percival] was eased to the right and the working day finally commenced at 1000Z with lunch at 1430Z and dinner at 2030Z. Daybreak was, at … around 1100Z*

The plan was to complete the final approach and initial landings during darkness, so there was little sleep to be had that night. We were determined to save as much as we could, should the Sir Percival be hit. Although only the reserve flight, we had worked with the ships officers to accommodate two, spread and armed Gazelles on the ships tiny

---

[20] "Proff: Steal or acquire an item or benefit from a situation" (Jolly1999 p344)

Bill O'Brien and Ken Priest preparing for a sortie

flight deck, ready for almost instant launch, in a manner that was almost safe! The ready crews started the night before the landings sleeping in immersion suits on the passageway floors immediately below the Flight Deck, together with the necessary technicians and aircraft handlers, in case the aircraft had to be launched rapidly.

Beachhead: The Battle of San Carlos Water

As we sailed into Falkland Sound in the early hours of Friday 21st May, we had prepared for flight and now sat in the aircraft 'locked and loaded', ready to be airborne in just a few minutes if required. I was in CZ with Bob Davenport and Bill O'Brien with Dolly Drummond in CM. A third crew were poised to deploy the other aircraft, CK, should one or both of us launch.

Monster was on deck, "it was dark with thick fog and eerily quiet, but it wasn't long before first light and the fog started to lift". Sir Percival, flying what had become her trademark pair of RFA colours, was certainly the first of the Amphibious Group, if not the first ship of the Task Force to enter San Carlos Water. As we glided past Fanning Head in the darkness, we could see explosions and tracer from the assault by a Special Boat Service (SBS) patrol on the Argentinean observation post (OP) they had detected

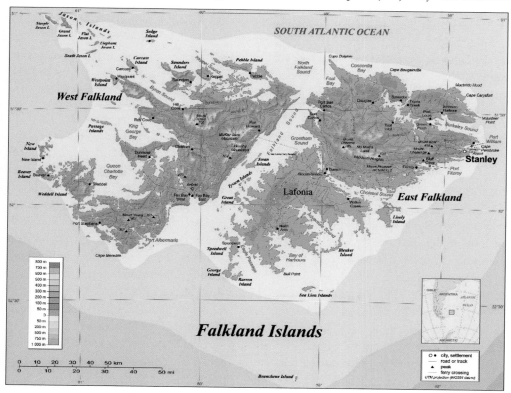

The Falkland Islands

45

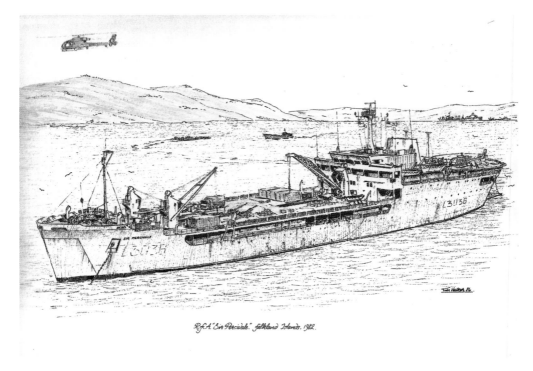

RfA "Sir Percivale" Falkland Islands. 1982.

Sketch by Tim Walker of Sir Percival, on D Day, operating in San Carlos Water

whilst covertly watching the chosen beachhead in the days before our arrival. Spirits were high. We had seen the assembled might of the Task Force with our own eyes and the approach that we had so feared had passed without mishap; surely, nothing could stop us now!

The tension of the approach initially gave way to a sense of anti-climax as the day broke bright and clear with no sign of enemy resistance. The Argentineans on Fanning Head had been quickly routed and there seemed to be no other enemy forces in the local area, so the Amphibious Task Group quickly got into what is commonly called, a 'volume offload'; i.e. to transfer ashore as much of the landing force and its supplies as you can, as quickly as you can. Fortunately, it was Sir Percival's tail ramp rather than deck that was in demand and we were able to keep the aircraft ranged, even though we stopped manning them. Things were going well for the Squadron. A Flight had been supporting operations on Fanning Head, B Flight were supporting Operations in and around San Carlos Water and C Flight was supporting the landings around Port San Carlos, whilst M Flight, in reserve and unused, was sulking! However, some disturbing traffic, soon began on the Squadron's radio net. Two aircraft from C Flight had been escorting SH moving equipment into the vicinity of Port San Carlos, where 3 Para's landing had fallen behind schedule and not allowed them the opportunity yet to clear the area. There had been a 'contact report' from a Sea King, and radio communication with CX had been lost. Communication was then lost with CY, which had gone to investigate. The third C Flight aircraft, flown by Robin Mackeig-Jones, an Army captain, was launched to try to locate them. After a short time, Robin reported that he had been unable to communicate with 3 Para and that just beyond Port San Carlos he had come under fire from a group of Argentineans who were retreating to the east. He had got away but was damaged and limping back to RFA Sir Galahad, upon which C Flight was based.

C Flight was now out of the fight, with two aircraft missing and the third damaged, so M Flight was committed to the battle and tasked to find out what was going on in Port San Carlos. This was the type of sortie we had talked and talked about, so we launched with little further briefing. As we approached Port San Carlos we could not contact 3 Para on the briefed frequency and, having previously agreed that failure to communicate with the ground troops was a 'no go', I decided to land near their battalion HQ and sort the problem out, before proceeding further.

This decision led to an incredible reunion. As we landed near some hastily dug positions, my rotor downwash blew away some maps and papers from the edge of a 3 Para mortar pit. As I disembarked from the aircraft, I saw a large and angry Para Sergeant closing on me, clearly intent on violence, until we recognised each other! It was Dave Robson, an old friend with whom I had been an army cadet many years before. Instead of killing me, which he later admitted to being his original intent, he quickly took me to the battalion HQ, where I established the correct frequency being used by 3 Para that day and was briefed that they thought the Argentinean troops retreating from Fanning Head were located somewhere to their east. We assumed that it was these troops who had engaged Robin and, with growing fear, the possibility that also they had shot down the missing aircraft. We resumed our patrol eastwards, to try and find any trace of our missing comrades. Certain that the Argentinean troops were to the north, we "skirmished along the southern shore of the water, one aircraft static, ready to provide suppressive fire with either rockets or GPMG, whilst the other moved to the next vantage point. We had not gone far when we spotted two aircrew, who later turned out to be an injured Eddy Candlish with the body of Andy Evans, on the far shore. They were at a small cluster of buildings called Port San Carlos Settlement, surrounded by locals but there was no sign of their aircraft. We informed 3 Para, who immediately sent a patrol to the settlement to provide help. We pushed on a little further but could not locate the other aircraft, which we had to presume lost to enemy action. The Argentineans appeared to be gone and it was not our job to pursue them, only to establish what was going on in Port San Carlos, which we felt we had done. My 'off the cuff' response to Will Scott about the role of Gazelles, made a few days earlier, had come back to haunt me.

As the story later unfolded, it turned out that the CX, crewed by Andy and Eddy, had been engaged by the Argentineans retreating from Fanning Head and shot down over the water. They managed to extricate themselves from the aircraft but Andy Evans, had been wounded by the fire. They were making towards the nearest shore when Eddy, who was assisting Andy, realised they were still being shot at and veered off towards Port San Carlos Settlement (see map below); the firing stopped just before they reached the shoreline. Now, as Eddy helped Andy from the water, he heard another aircraft and

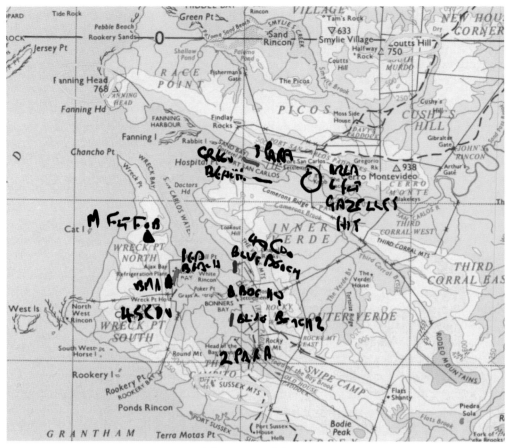

The scene of the crime

looked up just in time to watch helplessly as CY flew past the settlement and turned in the direction of the enemy. It soon came under fire and Eddy watched in horror as the crew compartment disintegrated and the aircraft crashed into a hillside, killing the occupants Ken Francis and Bret Giffin. Despite Eddy's best efforts, Andy died of his wounds soon after making it ashore.

That was M Flight's only significant engagement on the first day, but the calm of the anchorage soon changed. After a single Aeromacchi reconnaissance aircraft confirmed the presence of the Amphibious Task Group, an onslaught by the Argentine air force grew in scale and fury as the day wore on. As we watched helplessly from the deck of Sir Percival, wave after wave of attacks swept in, appearing suddenly, as they weaved through the hills at a suicidally low level, to avoid detection and the confuse the radar-controlled air defence missiles. Our first warning was often the sound of firing from the warships patrolling Falkland's Sound, the so called 'Goalkeepers'. As members of the landing force, we were spectators to this critical battle as the sailors fought back with every weapon they had. On Sir Percival, even the Captain had snatched up a rifle with which to fire at incoming aircraft from his bridge wing. Angus Horswill was duty pilot in our makeshift CP, to the rear of the Bridge:

"All I remember is passing on air raid warnings to the ship's Captain and watching from the bridge as Argentinean fast jets flew down San Carlos Water in a hail of anti-aircraft missiles and gunfire, trying to bomb the ships."

We again kept two aircraft manned, ready to launch at a moment's notice. Sitting in the cockpit Bill O'Brien looked over his shoulder:

"two A4s and a Mirage were flying low up the Water, pursued by volleys of missile smoke trails, BOFORS and GPMG fire, whilst the splash from their ordnance straddled ships in the anchorage."

Late in the morning, HMS Antrim limped into San Carlos water, with her air defence system crippled by a bomb that had passed through her magazine. Late in the day, HMS Argonaut, which had taken Antrim's place, also came into the anchorage being towed by HMS Plymouth. We were told that two bombs lay in her bowels; though unexploded one had so damaged the engine room that she had no power. To our consternation, the Rapier Air Defence posts for which C Flight had paid such a price to help get ashore were almost worthless at this critical stage, their delicate instrumentation having been disrupted by the violence of the South Atlantic storms through which we had sailed. It is the only time I have ever heard of a machine getting seasick! In all that day, there had been twelve waves of attack by a total of 72 aircraft. By the end of that first ferocious engagement of the battle, HMS Ardent had been sunk and four other

A Near Miss!

warships damaged as they fought courageously and successfully to protect the amphibious ships, which had escaped any damage. Fortunately, the Argentinean pilots had focused much of their attack on the escorts, at a heavy cost of 16 aircraft shot down.

By the evening, the strength of the attack had been enough to persuade the Amphibious Task Group commander, Commodore Michael Clapp, to keep in San Carlos Water only those ships being immediately unloaded, so plans to operate from the ships had to be quickly abandoned, lack of field equipment and tentage notwithstanding. We were ordered to quickly disembark our 3 aircraft and CP vehicle. Monster remembers:

Late that afternoon we were taken ashore by Seaking in a couple of sorties; FFR, trailer and passengers. Having been on the LSL since leaving Marchwood and considering the situation, I can seriously say I had never been so happy to get my feet on dry land but that didn't last long!

Thus, we found ourselves, with dusk falling and rain commencing, in a corner of the nascent Brigade Maintenance Area (BMA), with enough technical and material support to last for 24 hours and the knowledge that the Squadron had lost the lives of three of our comrades together with two, almost three, aircraft. What would tomorrow bring? The Squadron Commander visited us with a bottle of whiskey and encouraged us to grieve, good friends and close colleagues had been lost. Not quite 'Harry in the Night' but it helped.

At least we knew the facts. For wives and sweethearts back in UK it was not so clear. Most were shocked to hear the announcement that two Gazelles had been shot down with loss of crew but no other detail. They knew there were only 9 Gazelles down there so the odds were short and enquiry lines were overloaded. In M Flight, my own wife, Helen O'Brien and Debbie Horswill lived close together in Plymouth, but most wives were in Scotland and some elsewhere. None knew what had happened and could only hope and trust that if it were their man, they would have been told, or would they? By chance, the Squadron Administration Officer, a remarkable man called Richard Warren - left behind to look after the families and unaware of the detail of what was unfolding in the South Atlantic, had arranged for all the Plymouth based wives to meet the following day at the Squadron's base in Coypool, to record messages of love and support. Instead, he faced the grim task of informing them what had happened and providing support where it was needed.

Wives left in Arbroath and elsewhere, were even less well informed. For Carolyn Woods:

it all started getting scary when they landed at San Carlos; as the news was shocking in those days, there was not the overload of info that we get today! I remember the news kept saying "A small helicopter has been shot down and next of kin are being informed!" That's all they said all day the same thing. I suddenly thought "Oh my goodness we are up here with M Flight, but JC went down with 3 Cdo Bde so have they forgotten about us!" I phoned {the 45 Cdo] welfare and all they could say was "we don't know, we will find out and get back to you!" Those next few hours were awful, I was going frantic with fear, I'll never forget it, every time a car pulled up my heart sank! Then later that day the phone rang, and I remember crying, but it was with relief, as I knew they would never have phoned with bad news! But it was so sad to hear about the others.

Alyson Priest had arranged to take their baby girl and dog to collect Ken's mother from her home at Durrington and take her to the wedding of Ken's brother on Saturday 22nd of May. Ken was to have been his brother's Best Man.

We had heard on the Friday that two 'small helicopters' had been shot down with casualties. I tried in vain to find out who they were. Ken's Dad had also tried but, as he wasn't next of kin' wasn't able to get any names, he was just told not to worry! But it was very worrying and didn't exactly help the wedding celebrations. The wedding went ahead of course, there was nothing else to be done. I sat at the back of the church on my own, Ken's mum (mother of the groom) had to be persuaded to go at all and got quite cross with me! I had been intending to stay a few days but decided to return home to Plymstock on Sunday by which time I think the names of those who had been lost had been announced.

In the event Sir Percival had not sailed and, apart from some early raids, the following day became eerily quiet. So, we re-embarked to set about readjusting ourselves now that it was clear that we would have to operate ashore, from a forward operating base (FOB), for the foreseeable future. The Squadron Commander had decided that C Flight, with only one aircraft remaining must be reconstituted and ordered M Flight to transfer an aircraft to C Flight to achieve this. I protested vigorously, since this would jeopardise our ability to field a tactical pair, the need and procedure for which we had spent long hours discussing during the voyage; the logic being that a flight needed three aircraft, in order to be able to guarantee two in the air. However, I was firmly told that, for understandable reasons, Peter was determined to get C Flight back in the saddle and would not be swayed. Sorting out these reorganisations kept me on the ground all day, but the Flight was busy, principally with communication tasks. The first sortie that day was flown by Will Scott and Ken Priest and the atmosphere on the flight deck was tense. After the previous day's misadventures, some wondered if this could be the last they saw of Will and Ken and there is no doubt that those two were thinking the same. Just before they took off, we received instructions that each aircraft should carry body bags (just in case) and Monster was dispatched to get some before Will and Ken took off. In Will's words:

> *We all sat uneasily, waiting for his return, no one wanting to make eye contact with us, as we contemplated our immediate future. The tension was broken by the arrival of the body bags and Monster casually saying to me "Do you want to put these on now sir, to save time later?". Everyone instantly fell about laughing at this realisation of Royal Marine 'gallows humour', something that constantly helped us all get by.*

Later, Terry Waldron delivered CK to C flight on Sir Galahad. There was no one on the flight deck so he just landed, shutdown and signed off the aircraft logbook.

I then went in search of somebody that could take over the tech log. I found them all gathered in one of the mess decks and could see that I had walked in on their wake for the lost crews. I just laid the tech log down on the table and slowly backed out. The next problem was how to get back to Sir Percival. As luck would have it a mexeflote was just then passing the ship. I stuck out my thumb and the mexeflote pulled over to give me a lift.

Our first FOB

After a quiet start on the 23rd May, the air attacks renewed. The 'Goalkeepers', did a fantastic job, soaking up a lot of the attacks and forcing others to come in very low, which made their targeting difficult and, as it was revealed later, often did not allow their bombs time to arm before they struck, no doubt saving many lives. However, the logistic ships, vulnerably sitting at anchor were now becoming the main target so, despite the affection we had developed for Sir Percival, it was time to move ashore permanently. I was determined to find a FOB location away from the BMA, which was as much of a target as the ships in the anchorage. I eventually found a bowl, high up a re-entrant on the hills to the southern side of San Carlos Water, which offered some protection. It was only accessible by air but away from the main foci of the battle, which suited us fine.

As a bonus, a Rapier firing post was positioned not far from the top of the re-entrant which allowed Monster to think "we've got our own air defence up the hill". However, their first missile went off like a rogue fire work causing more danger to us than the Skyhawk against which it had been launched. Angus Horswill was returning to the FOB:

I remember watching a nearby Rapier battery launching a missile, which went rogue. Believe me, this was far more frightening than the Argentine fighters, it was doing multiple low level loops and flying at chest height, totally out of control, until it finally ran out of propellant and embedded itself in the ground. Fortunately, it had a very small warhead and didn't cause much damage upon impact. Apparently, the guidance system for the Rapier system was sensitive and hadn't liked the treatment it had received during its deployment. Despite this they appeared to be remarkably effective and I saw a number of aircraft fall prey to them.

I remember that I had been doubtful of the military inclination of our non-Commando trained REME aircraft technicians, but this quickly proved unfounded when I found that, under air attack, their technical expertise was surpassed only by their ability to dig trenches! However, some military skills were lacking. On one occasion, when a couple of aircraft appeared over the Sussex Mountain ridge, everyone was diving into trenches with the exception of Charlie Walker who, standing on a small knoll, looking in the direction of the oncoming aircraft, announced in an authoritative voice, "FRIENDLIES!". Seconds, later, a couple of bombs went off on the other side of San Carlos Water. Charlie very quickly joined, the rest of the flight in the trenches, where it was unkindly suggested by some that he should go on an aircraft recognition course if and when he got back to UK!

The air raids by now seemed to have a settled into a pattern. A "Yellow" alert was broadcast when aircraft were reported to be 'en route' and "Amber" close to their expected time on target. A radio warning "Air Raid Red", or sometimes simply the sound of rapid firing by the air defence piquet' guns out in Falkland Sound, signalling an imminent attack and providing the cue for all helicopters and landing craft to head as rapidly as possible for cover in the inlets and folds of ground around the anchorage. Terry Waldron:

had just departed from [HMS] Fearless heading south towards the Sussex Mountain ridge when we saw, I believe it was four, Argentinean mirages appear from over the ridge heading in our direction. My first thought was, why me I'm just a small helicopter. At the same time JC was encouraging me to get lower and get out of the way. I pushed the right pedal as far as it would go and the cyclic forward and left. This caused the aircraft to sideslip and descend rapidly. The Mirages over flew us and it became obvious the target was not us but HMS Fearless. However, a new manoeuvre ticked off the list that day! On another occasion, JC and I were flying east along the coast towards Port San Carlos, when we heard 'air raid warning red' over the radio. We were close to a small re-entrant I had seen earlier, where we could take cover. I carried out a steep left-hand turn into the re-entrant, only to find it was already occupied by a Seaking! To avoid a collision, I had to carry out a violent quick stop and managed to come to a halt only a few feet from the other aircraft. I looked across at the Seaking to see two pilots with big grins on their faces! One of them transmitted on the chat frequency a simple "Hello, another lucky day". After a while we asked the Navy pilots whether they had heard an all clear. Neither of us had so I suggested that they pull up into a hover and have a look around. Their counter suggestion was, it might be a good idea if we went into a high hover and have a look around, as we were a smaller target!

We felt for the landing craft crews because we could travel much faster than they, whilst the slow moving mexeflotes, along with the anchored ships, had no option but to grit their teeth, bear the onslaught and hope for the best. The situation was not always clear, and nerves sometimes became frayed. On one occasion, on the squadron net, a testy pilot demanded clarification of the air raid state, "was it Red or Amber?" The ever calm Senior Pilot, Andrew Eames, broke the tension, "hard to say to be honest, not really red, not really yellow, more a sort of burnt ochre"!

We watch the stricken last hours of HMS Antelope from our FOB

It was inevitable that ships would be hit and that evening we were saddened to see HMS Antelope, our escort during the first stage of the journey south, limp into the sound, smoking gently, with an unexploded 500-pound bomb buried deep within her, which some brave souls were attempting to defuse whilst the rest of the crew were assembled on deck. Sadly, the bomb exploded, killing the bomb disposal expert working on it and starting fires that spread uncontrollably through the ship, forcing it to be abandoned.

Like many others around the anchorage, Monster, who was on watch, witnessed the demise of HMS Antelope,

"it started off as a small plume of smoke, giving the impression it was all under control, then there was an explosion and a raging fire; the following day her back broke and she went down into Davey Jones's locker."

The next day the air assault continued, seemingly unabated, with both Sir Galahad and Sir Lancelot being hit. Thankfully, on both occasions, the bombs failed to explode but the vulnerability of the amphibious ships was clear to see. For ourselves, it soon became clear that the greatest threats to our secluded little FOB, were the stray rounds and overshoots of our own people engaging enemy aircraft, which often flew low along the hillside, with everything from missiles to pistols.

On Tuesday 25th May, we were placed in direct support of 3 Para and tasked to reconnoitre north towards Coutts Hill, where, it was believed, the Argentine troops who had engaged C Flight had withdrawn. We flew as a tactical pair, myself with JC as my observer and Will Scott with Ken Priest flying as wingman. We used the same fire and manoeuvre skirmishing technique that we had undertaken previously in Port San Carlos, as we cautiously approached our objective. However, after two hours of tense patrolling, we could do no more than inform 3 Para that, wherever else they were, there were no Argentinean troops on Coutts Hill.

Whilst the air attack on the anchorage had abated, we learned that evening that another of the guardships, HMS Coventry had been sunk and a supply ship, the Atlantic Conveyor had been badly damaged by an Exocet missile, both with significant loss of life. The latter was a logistic disaster also, with the loss of three Chinook and five Wessex helicopters, leading to significant reshaping of the land scheme of manoeuvre.

More mundanely, on the evening of 26th, Bill and I were surprised to learn that we were to be given a check ride on PNG by Peter Cameron and the Squadron QHI, Rodney Helme, neither of whom had previously flown with PNG. We met them at the B Flight FOB in Ajax Bay and then, individually, conducted short trips with Peter, complete with helmet mounted goggles, in the left-hand seat whist Rodney, using handheld PNG, sat in the back. Bill and I had been getting on tolerably well, so we thought, with our over water training sorties and we felt confident. However, the 'check ride' was my first overland sortie with real PNG and transpired to be a sobering experience. Shortly after we took off, to fly a low-level circuit of San Carlos Water, my

PNG lost focus and all I could see was a green blur rushing past at alarming speed. I reported this to Peter and started to climb to a safe altitude but Peter, an experienced and accomplished pilot (but who, I was conscious, was flying on PNG for the first time in his life), said everything was fine, took control and continued the sortie at low level, whilst I tried to sort out my own optics. My equanimity was not helped by a series of warning calls from Rodney in the back of the aircraft. Seriously unnerved by all this and with slightly better focus, I took back control and continued the sortie, until the blur returned. This time, I said nothing and climbed straight to safe altitude, before coming off PNG and recovering to Ajax Bay in standard fashion. Feeling pretty shaken, I vacated the seat for Bill to have his ride. Bill also thought his check had gone badly but we had survived intact and since our 'checkers' knew no better, so we were authorised to fly 'PNG - Op Corporate only'. However, at that moment, I do not think either of us thought that we might ever want to use PNG again!

Just before dusk, the final Argentinean air raid for the day struck the BMA in Ajax Bay, killing five personnel and wounding 27, whilst also causing significant losses to equipment and supplies. Having delivered its bombs and seeking to evade the volleys of fire from the anchorage, one Skyhawk flew low, directly up the re-entrant that led to our position. We watched, with equal fascination and horror, as the Skyhawk raced towards us, pursued by a swarm of tracer and a sea slug missile! Fortunately for us, the tracer did not have the range and the sea slug did not have the legs to catch it. Clearly sensing that this one was about to get away, Martin Walkinshaw, decided to have a go himself and, shouting defiance, did a passable Rambo impersonation, firing a GPMG from the hip at the jet as it approached and flew low directly overhead. Ken Priest, possibly more in hope than expectation, was doing the same with a short barrelled, low velocity, sub-machine gun (SMG). We could clearly see rounds impacting the Skyhawk and it seemed to start trailing fuel as it banked hard to pass low over the crest of the hill. Despite our professional admiration for the pilots daring and skill, we all hoped that this was one aircraft that would not return to base. On behalf of Martin, we reported a 'kill' but the claim was summarily dismissed! However, history has revealed evidence of a Skyhawk pilot who, realising he was losing fuel and unlikely to make it back to Argentina, decided to eject over the dry land of West Falklands, an area then still in Argentine hands.

Martin Walkinshaw took part in the SAMA 2002 Pilgrimage together with Peter Cameron and other members of the Squadron and, to his satisfaction, made a trip to West Falkland to see for himself his claimed kill. Peter later reported that Martin brought back a piece of the Skyhawk complete with holes that may well have been caused by GPMG rounds, to prove his claim.

Evidence of Martin Walkinshaw's 'kill'?

Martin was not the only member of the Flight to have a claim disputed. On the second day of the battle, Angus Horswill with Bob Davenport as his observer, was moving an artillery officer to the top end of peninsula that separated San Carlos Water and the Falkland Sound, to recce a site for a Rapier anti-aircraft post. After a hairy drop off, on sloping ground below the crest, they returned to collect their charge at a prearranged time:

However, there was no sign of our passenger. I suspected that he was less than impressed with my previous sloping ground technique and may have decided that he had a better chance of survival on the flatter ground on the top of the ridge despite [the threat from] the Argentinian Air Force. Sure enough, we found him patiently waiting for us on the flat ground at the top of the ridge where I carried out a normal landing, into wind facing west and looking out across Falkland Sound. Just then, about a mile offshore, a diesel submarine did a dramatic emergency surfacing, where the hull angle is about 45 degrees, most of the hull leaves the water before it crashes back in a and large spray of water. It immediately dived back under the surface to submerge. On the way south we had done extensive equipment recognition of all the various Argentinian ships and were told that any diesel submarine we saw had to be Argentinian as all our subs were nuclear. As far as I was concerned, I had just seen an enemy submarine trying to get into San Carlos Water to attack our shipping. So, I sent a full contact report on the Squadron radio net but, minutes later the Senior Pilot announced on the radio to cancel the contact report and said that I had transmitted it in error. To say I was 'pissed off' would be an understatement and after returning to the flight location received the usual banter from the rest of the flight who treated it as a huge joke at my expense.

However, ten years later, as a commercial pilot, Angus met another pilot who, in a previous life had been in the FAA and told him this little tale:

It transpired that his best mate in the RN, who he trained with at Dartmouth, became a submariner and eventually the Captain of HMS ONYX, an Oberon class diesel submarine that was adapted to insert special forces ashore whilst submerged; he was in command when she secretly deployed to the Falklands. What he believed I had witnessed was her emergency surface after hitting an uncharted reef in Falkland sound. A large chunk of which became embedded in the hull and was only removed after dry docking on return to the UK. Obviously, somebody wanted this to remain a secret at the time.

A Close-Run Thing: Goose Green

Under pressure from London, 3 Commando Brigade began to expand the perimeter of the beachhead. 2 Para were to move south to raid a strong Argentinean position at Goose Green. Meanwhile, using the limited helicopter lift available, 42 Commando would be flown to Mount Kent, once landing sites were secured by SF, whilst 45 Commando and 3 Para were to 'yomp' and 'tab' respectively from Port San Carlos, towards Stanley.

On the morning of the 27th, we heard that 2 Para had moved forward during the night to lie up at Camilla Creek House in preparation for an attack on Goose Green the following night. M Flight, together with two Scouts from B Flight, were to be in direct support for the duration of the battle. Andrew Eames had gone forward with the 2 Para HQ, to be an aviation liaison officer (LO), to avoid a repeat the communication failure that had occurred in Port San Carlos on the first day of the landings, as well as to coordinate to best effect the little aviation support that was available. Jeff Niblett (Commanding B Flight), John Glaze, Dick Nunn and Bill Belcher were crewing the Scouts, whilst I, with Dolly Drummond, Angus Horswill and Bob Davenport were in the Gazelles. The focus of our effort had shifted mainly to do what we could to supplement the lift capacity of the few available SH, rather than reconnaissance, and our task that day was to ferry supplies, particularly ammunition, to boost that which the Paras had been able to carry for themselves on their night move. As we needed all possible space and payload, we removed the GPMG mounts for that task and I am not sure they were ever refitted.

Initially, we landed on Sussex Mountain, recently occupied by 2 Para, where we could study the ground and work out how best to reach Camilla Creek House (just north of Darwin) over the flat terrain, without compromising 2 Para's presence. As it happened, compromise did not matter because, as we learned later, the BBC World Service announced that an attack on Goose Green was imminent! From up on the mountain, the ground we needed to cover looked exceedingly flat and exposed. To add to our concerns, we heard that a Sea Harrier had been shot down, whilst attacking the Argentine positions at Goose Green, amply demonstrating the effectiveness of their anti-aircraft defences. After a short while, we managed to identify a network of folds in the ground that we could use to make reasonably discrete and protected passage, if we kept low enough. To achieve this, there was no question of using underslung loads; everything would have to be internal. For the rest of the day we tried to place as much materiel as we could at

Camila Creek House, where 2 Para were laid up, to prepare them for the planned attack. Angus Horswill:

> ... *spent the entire day flying ammunition forward at well above the allowed maximum weight at extreme low level and I lost count of the number of trips I made. The loading technique was to cram as much ammunition as was physically possible into the aircraft and then pull power to see if you could produce sufficient lift to do a running take off, where the skids remain in contact with the ground as you slide forward until "transitional" airflow produced sufficient lift to get airborne. If the aircraft wouldn't budge ammunition was offloaded until it would. At the drop off point a zero-speed low power landing was carried out on a patch of suitably flat ground.*

I remember being very frustrated by 2 Para's apparent lack of preparation before they moved forward. We were sent to gather mortar ammunition had been left disbursed in mortar lines rather than, concentrated for easy collection, so that we wasted valuable time, shutting down the aircraft and scouring abandoned mortar pits, rather than hauling prepared loads. It was only later that I learned that netted loads, ready to be flown forward from Ajax Bay, had been destroyed during the bombing of the BMA the previous evening. A combination of other vital tasks and the flat terrain meant that SH, with their much higher profiles, were not used to support 2 Para during daylight but, that night, they flew three guns from 8 Battery, together with ammunition, to a gun line near Camilla Creek House.

With both our aircraft committed to this task, there was nothing for those left back at the FOB to do, except to frustratedly "hang around the flight CP and wait for news". Charlie Walker later recalled,

> *After the events of the first few days I think all the guys on the ground staff were a bit on tenterhooks when the aircrew were away on task. Always good to hear the sound of the Astazou[21] as the aircraft were on their way back. The easiest time was probably when we were actually working on the aircraft!*

At 0230 on 28th May, 2 Para began their attack, with the aim to secure all objectives, except the settlement itself, in darkness. However, progress was slow and by first light, the advance had still not reached Darwin Hill and Boca House, both of which dominated the approaches to Goose Green, and the Paras were becoming fixed by small arms and artillery fire.

---

[21] Astazou is the name of the gas turbine engine that powers the Gazelle

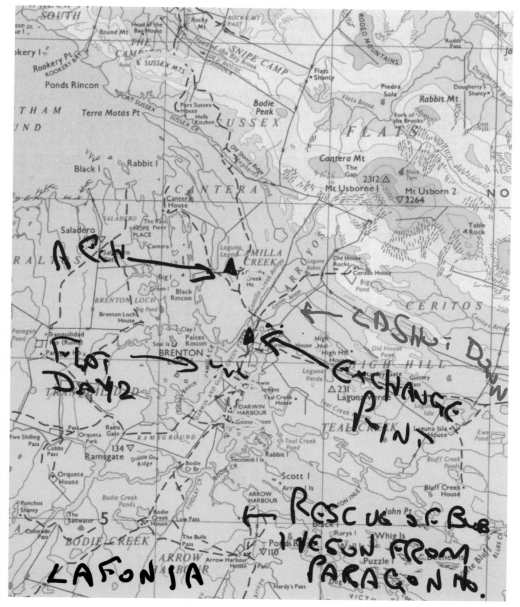

The Battle for Goose Green

They were also perilously low on ammunition - the two mortars had run out by the time we became engaged. Ken Priest was now my observer whist Dolly Drummond was back with Bill O'Brien in the second aircraft. At first light, together with the two Scouts, we moved to a temporary forward base at Camilla Creek House; Terry Waldron and JC also moved forward with us, to allow for crew changes without wasting time in returning to the FOB. Bill O'Brien, was seeing the ground for the first time, *in order to get there, we flew along a shallow fold in the ground, as low as we could. It took us right in front of the artillery gun line that had been flown in during the night. The guns were busy, and the airframe flexed and shook with every shot … Dolly's face was a picture!*

The Paras had established an exchange point for ammunition supply and casualty evacuation (CASEVAC), in the vicinity of Burntside House as I recall. Andrew Eames had positioned himself there, to try and coordinate our aviation efforts. He had an A41 VHF radio on the Squadron's allocated frequency but, applying lessons learned around San Carlos, when moving into the battle area, we needed our single VHF radio to monitor the 2 Para frequency, to follow the progress of the battle and identify from where threats might come, rather than the Squadron net. Working as a pair this was not a problem as we could monitor both and transfer information on the AM chat net. But working alone, as was becoming increasingly the case, this made communication with Andrew difficult. In later battles, our LOs carried a UHF radio to overcome this problem. Our main task now was to fly ammunition (particularly mortar rounds) forward, often delivering directly to the mortar line, and taking serious casualties straight to the dressing station in Ajax Bay.

On one occasion, Bill arrived during an enemy barrage. The Paras were sensibly hunkered down in their trenches and seemed oblivious to the presence of an aircraft full of precious ammunition only meters behind them. Bill could see the explosions and feel the concussion through the airframe but all he could hear was the high-pitched whine of the Gazelle's engine. He simply couldn't attract the Paras' attention and was thinking maybe he ought to fly away when, Andrew Eames, armed with a pistol, a green beret and an A41 radio appeared, picked up a pick helve and walked round the trenches batting the Paras on their helmets and gesticulating towards the aircraft. They then stirred themselves

Delivering ammo to the front line

Camila Creek House

and began to move towards the aircraft to unload it, at which point Andrew decided he wanted to have a word with Bill and began to move towards the aircraft. Bill was hoping Andrew's beret didn't blow off and that he would remember he had an A41 radio with a long whip antenna on his back. Andrew's beret stayed put but he forgot about the antenna and, despite Bill's frantic signaling, entered the rotor disc. The top of the antenna was severed by the rotors and sent arcing upwards but, as Andrew leaned toward the cockpit window to talk, it plunged back to earth and literally stuck into the ground by his feet. Without missing a beat Andrew said, "you'd better f*** off Sgt O'Brien, they're using bloody bows and arrows now!"

From outset, with the loads being carried, power margins were minimal or non-existent, so advanced techniques for take offs and landings were the norm. Nobody had the time or inclination to weigh anything we carried, so the torque meter (measuring the strain being placed on the transmission system) became sole arbiter of what was possible and what was not. Terry Waldron, accompanied by JC, was continuing his steep learning curve. The first time they landed at the BMA, to collect vital ammunition, JC jumped out of the aircraft to assist in the loading, whilst Terry, as he had been taught in pilot training, set about calculating how many boxes he could carry and stay within his authorised AUM. During his calculations:

I was hit on the back of the head by a box of ammunition. JC had loaded the aircraft all the way to the roof. He jumped in and suggested it might be good idea to get, going. I applied power but the aircraft refused to leave the ground. It did however become light on the skids, so I applied a little forward cyclic and we started to ski across the wet grass. As translational lift kicked in, I nursed the aircraft into the air, narrowly avoiding some nearby tents. Another new flying technique learned that day!

Now loaded with ammunition, they headed into the battle area for the first time. JC's heart was pumping overtime, as we were not the first aircraft there and the news of the battle had been coming back to the CP, so we were well aware of what lay ahead. We found the Para's logistic base [exchange point] and, as we flew in, I saw the Para dead laid out wrapped in their ponchos. As we started to off load their ammunition, I had this extreme urge to go over to the last man who was on his side as if asleep with his poncho wrapped around him to tell him to wake up; I climbed back into the aircraft and we carried on with the war.

Meanwhile, on the 2 Para radio command net I heard the commander of A Company passing a warning to H Jones, the CO, who was leading his Tac HQ to personally attack a trench on Darwin Hill, shortly followed by the call "Sunray[22] is down" when Jones was mortally wounded. Things seemed to be going from bad to worse.

Ken and I were at Camilla Creek House awaiting the next task, when two Pucaras appeared suddenly, seemingly heading straight towards our position. I dived into a ditch to take cover, telling Ken to do the same but, remaining steadfastly on his feet, he announced that they were not after us but had locked onto the two B Flight Scouts that were moving forward as a tactical pair (to CASEVAC Jones, as we later learned), and had been caught in the open.

The Pucara is a twin-engine aircraft with a low stall speed, designed for counter insurgency. With full flap and in strong winds it can almost hover, like a bird of prey. It was a vastly different proposition to the fast jets against which we had trained in fighter evasion tactics. As we had been trained to do, the two Scouts split, Jeff right, taking him towards Camilla Creek and fire support, Dick left, which, sadly, took him away. Both were flying for their lives and losing kinetic energy with every low-level manoeuvre, the danger of which we had never been taught in Army pilot training. The Pucaras, with flaps down and close to stall speed were closely matching the manoeuvres of our Scouts, but with the advantage of altitude, which gave them potential energy. After some remarkable flying, guided by a running commentary on the position of the attacker from John Glaze,

Argentine Pucara through a cam net

[22] Radio codename for commanding officer

All that remained of Scout DR

in the back of the aircraft, Jeff made it into the safety of an umbrella of fire from Camilla Creek, which drove off his attacker. Dick was not so fortunate. Ken Priest and I watched helplessly as Dick's aircraft disappeared into dead ground, now with both the Pucaras pursuing him.

Then, as suddenly as they had arrived, the Argentinean aircraft were flying away but we could see an ominous plume of smoke, not far from where the Scout had gone out of view. Fearing the worst, Ken and I, quickly prepared to launch, to check the situation. As we ran to the aircraft, JC ran to join us, jumping into the back as we headed towards the pall of smoke. Approaching the scene, we could see aircraft wreckage and what looked like one person kneeling down giving first aid to another; our hopes were raised.

I dropped Ken and JC with a medical kit and re-launched to provide overwatch of the sight, with all rockets armed and the crazy idea that I could fight them off, if the Pucaras reappeared. As JC ran forward the situation became clear, "It was Billy, on his own, with his legs at an extreme angle to the rest of his body. Both his lower legs were shattered, like a butcher's shop, where do you start?". Ken signalled me to return, in order to tell me that Dick was dead in the burnt-out aircraft and Belcher's legs were almost severed - we needed a stretcher to move him. We agreed that it would be better to move Belcher on a stretcher in a Scout, so, I left Ken and JC to manage his injuries as best they could, whilst I went to find Jeff, whose Scout would provide a better means of recovery, and a stretcher.

The close-knit family nature of the Corps once again came to the fore. JC had previously served with Bill Belcher on a ship's detachment:

Billy and I had been shipmates on HMS Ashanti back in 1975, however the need was to focus on the immediate. A collection of triangular bandages gathered together his lower legs and the door frame from the Scout became a splint. Billy was extremely pale and covered in sweat but managed to sit up and ask me for some Morphine. I went to find mine from around my neck as I could not find Billy's. My morphine was a glass phial stuck to a doctor tongue stick. I soon realised what the stain on my tee shirt for the past few days was!! The glass had broken hence the stain. I turned to Ken and used his and went to mark Billy's forehead. My pen didn't work on his pale and sweaty forehead so, I produced a permanent lumacolour and marked his head with "M" and the time. As he laid back, Billy says to me "Thanks J C mine wasn't working!" So, Billy now had two doses of Morphine in quick succession; out came the marker and Billy's forehead "note pad" had yet more notes. He did not think it was so funny a few days later when I visited him on the Uganda the marker would not wash off.

Meanwhile, I found Jeff and John at Camilla Creek House, where they had landed and were, understandably, going into shock. To their immense credit, they put their own trauma aside and relaunched to fly with me back to the crash site to evacuate Belcher.

Since JC, had administered morphine he went with the casualty in the Scout, whilst Ken re-embarked with me. We then flew as a pair to the dressing station in Ajax Bay and, as soon as JC had handed Belcher over to the medics, we picked him up and flew back to re-join the battle.

After a few more sorties, with weather diminishing, night closing and crews both physically and mentally exhausted, I decided that it was time for M Flight to quit the field. Bill O'Brien and Terry Waldron wanted to go on, but I overruled them. Two scouts from 656 Sqn, had arrived with fresh crews to relieve B Flight and were planning to continue to provide support but they too soon had to stop, when deteriorating weather forced one of them into an instrument recovery to San Carlos Water, through cloud, with no radar, relying on being talked down by Peter Cameron.

Terry Waldron was flying on the last rotation of the day out of Camilla Creek, in company with the other aircraft, flown by Bill and Dolly;

We had two wounded and the acting CO (might have been one of the company commanders) on board. Just before departure we were informed that an Argentinean Chinook may have landed just over the knoll in front of us. The only way out was a low-level downwind departure. Not an insurmountable problem, I was getting quite happy with running the aircraft along the grass until I achieved translational lift. But this time I didn't have the luxury of a flat field of grass. There was tussock grass everywhere and it proved to be a bumpy departure!

That night, as I sat on the hillside considering our situation, it seemed we were at a low point. Several ships had been sunk, the BMA bombed, and the Brigade was running low on supplies. The Paras, when we had last seen them, seemed bogged down and, as a Squadron, we had now lost 3 aircraft, 20 percent of our force. The unthinkable, suddenly occurred to me; if fortunes did not change quickly, we might come second!

At first light the next morning, still with this thought in my mind, I was heading back to Goose Green. Bob Davenport was once again my observer, with Will Scott and Ken Priest in the other aircraft - all of us were apprehensive, given the events of the previous day. Though we didn't know it, the tide of the battle had begun to turn soon after we departed. Chris Keeble, the 2 Para second in command, now acting as CO – had reset the plan of attack. Darwin Hill and Boca House were secured, and 2 Para had begun to establish control of the battlefield. By the time we arrived, at Camilla Creek House, the situation was transformed and by mid-morning the Argentine garrison had surrendered. But first, Will and Ken were tasked to return to 2 Para's previous position on Sussex Mountains (south end of San Carlos Water) and bring down more mortars, as 2 Para had only been able to carry two tubes when they marched south. Arriving at the apparently abandoned position, Will shut down and, together with Ken, started to search on foot, eventually finding a couple of sleepy Paratroopers who were acting as 'rear party'. Between them, they loaded the mortar tubes into nets, so they could be flown as an "underslung" load.

We were told that the surrender was taking place and that we would be required to transport the two senior Argentine Officer's at Goose Green - one Army Commander and one Air Force Commander – to our Brigade HQ back in San Carlos Water. Flying into the settlement, over what had been the previous day's battle lines, presented quite a sight, with over 1000 the Argentine personnel drawn up in ranks, their helmets and weapons stockpiled in accordance with the terms of the surrender agreement. We were told that the plan was fly the two senior officers back to our Brigade Headquarters' where attempts would be made to convince them to go to Port Stanley and tell the Argentine Commander (Gen Menendez) that further resistance was futile and that there was no dishonour in surrender. To support this idea, they were to be afforded as much dignity as possible and be flown separately, in comfort, which meant that we had quickly to re-role both aircraft to fit passenger seats. As a final note, we were told it had been agreed that they were being allowed to keep their sidearms! Ken Priest was not at all happy at the prospect of carrying an armed Argentine Air Force Commander. As far as he was concerned this was a POW with a gun. Will noticed that "Ken pulled out his 9 mm pistol and held it out of sight but ready to shoot the Argentine Brigadier at the first sign of hostility!" As it was, we flew back to Brigade HQ without incident; my own passenger almost seemed relieved that it was over. Brigadier Thompson met the aircraft personally and that was the last we saw of them. We heard later that they had refused to go back to Menendez so, presumably, they were disarmed and became normal POW's.

Thereafter, the primary task was to evacuate the casualties of both sides. However, residents of Goose Green reported that they had seen a parachute deploy from the downed Harrier the day before and that it appeared to have landed in Lafonia, to the south of the settlement. After some discussion with Andrew Eames, I agreed to send

Will and Ken to try to locate and recover the downed pilot. We had no idea if there were still Argentine troops out there and scant knowledge of where the downed pilot might be. The squadron had already lost two aircraft by probing into uncleared areas and, in these similar circumstances, tasking a lone aircraft was deeply troubling. However, with, only two aircraft available, and a multitude of tasks, there seemed no alternative. We agreed that Will and Ken should initially head out over the water on the west side of the Goose Green isthmus and then work their way inland to check out two derelict farmhouses, where it was possible a downed pilot may have sought refuge. They were to search for no more than 45 minutes and then pull out if they had not located him. Will takes up the story:

Heading very gingerly and at no more than a hover taxi into a shallow gully, we headed towards the now derelict Paragon House. At first, we saw nothing and dropped back into the cover of the ravine. We decided to try an approach from the other side, using another ravine, staying in dead ground as much as possible. We were about to pull back again with nothing seen, when Ken said he thought he'd seen a mini flare; then, after a pause for reflection, added that it could have been tracer bouncing upwards, which could look remarkably similar. A tense moment as we looked at each other - which was it? At that very moment, the downed pilot emerged from the long grass only 100 meters away. It was obvious to us who he was, but not knowing of the surrender at Goose Green, he had feared initially that we were Argentineans and had remained hidden, watching us carefully for about ten minutes. With a much-relieved Squadron Leader Bob Iveson on board, we flew back to Ajax Bay as quickly as possible, to deliver him to the field hospital.

Later in the day Terry Waldron and JC were sent to collect Robert Fox, the war correspondent, who had accompanied 2 Para through the battle, and move him to the Brigade HQ, where he could file his report. Shortly after they landed, Fox emerged from a house and started to hop and skip towards the aircraft, with such vigour that the earflaps of his winter hat were bouncing up-and-down. JC started to dismount as quickly as he could to try and prevent the untimely beheading of a civilian reporter. Unfortunately, Fox was too quick and, still hopping and skipping, entered under the rotor disc. Terry managed to tilt the disc sufficiently to avoid disaster whist JC firmly took charge of Fox, got him in the aircraft and handed him a headset. Fox was high on adrenaline and, from the smell, some whiskey too! He talked incessantly during the flight, reliving what he had seen over the last few days. After landing at the Brigade HQ, JC opened the door and before any more could be said, Fox jumped from the aircraft and started running towards the HQ tents. To the amusement of the crew, Fox got about five steps from the aircraft before the headset that he was still wearing, itself still attached to the aircraft, jerked him backwards and onto the ground!

It had been a busy, eventful, and traumatic few days but fortunately M flight had come through it unscathed and the eventual, hard won victory of 2 Para at Goose Green eradicated my doubts about the eventual outcome. However, it was clear that there were still hard days ahead and that M flight had a full part to play in them.

Into the Misty Mountains: The Breakout from the Beachhead

During the battle for Goose Green, 45 Commando and 3 Para had begun their epic yomp/tab across the north of East Falkland and had secured Douglas Settlement and Teal Inlet, respectively. On 30th May, we were told to move our FOB to Teal Inlet, at the same time supporting 45 Commando who, by now, were continuing their advance from Douglas Settlement and moving towards Teal Inlet. Angus Horswill and I flew a reconnaissance mission to find a suitable location for our new home to be, with John Hopkinson and Ian Mellor to advise and assist. There were several agricultural buildings suitable for accommodation in the small settlement at Teal Inlet but, having been first to arrive, 3 Para had bagged most and the best of them. Luckily, we found a small hay barn that would provide relatively warm dry accommodation, which the owners were willing to let us use. As Teal Inlet was rapidly becoming filled with new arrivals there was no time to lose, if we wanted to hang onto our barn, so we began our move immediately.

Our FOB equipment was moved as underslung loads by two Sea Kings with those not engaged in flying duties travelling as passengers. Angus Horswill remembers watching as the grossly overloaded CP trailer, containing our meagre stock of tentage jettisoned, leaving a trail of discarded canvas across the landscape, so it was fortunate

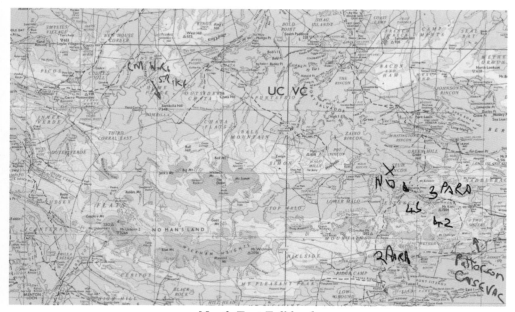

North East Falklands

Supporting 45 Commando's 'Yomp' from Douglas Settlement

that, at Teal Inlet, we were accommodated in an outbuilding. Whilst Mellor and Hopkinson sorted out the FOB, we started to ferry forward the bergens that 45 had left stockpiled at Douglas Settlement, having been told that SH would lift them forward. In the event, no SH were available so, knowing what it would be like to lie up without the comforts those bergens would hold, we scurried back and forth for the rest of the day, trying to move as many as possible with our two aircraft. Angus Horswill and Bob Davenport were flying one of them:

We were tasked to move underslung loads of bergens belonging to a Company of 45 Commando from Douglas to Teal Inlet. But, with no ground party at the pick-up point, we had to land, shut down and put the bergens in cargo nets. A strop was then laid out along the ground and I repositioned the aircraft over the end of strop with its end near the cargo hook. Bob then attached the strop to the hook and got back into the aircraft. I then came into a hover and positioned the aircraft over the net before lifting it. It was a slow process, but we eventually managed to shift all of them.

Other companies were not so lucky. As night fell, we had not shifted all the bergens, but we had done all we could to aid our fellow Royal Marines.

Meanwhile, the settlement manager had become annoyed by marines chopping down wood in a nearby copse, protesting that it took years to grow woodland in the Falkland Islands. It seemed that the marines were not too happy either and retorted along the lines: "Do you want these f****** islands back or not?" A little bit of 'hearts and minds' was required to calm things down, so I sent Will Scott to try and placate the Settlement Manager. Much later, Will admitted that when he went to the manager's house, he was offered a square meal and a bath. Feeling guilty (he claims) Will accepted both, then crept sheepishly back into the barn, feeling exceptionally clean and well-nourished and wisely keeping his good fortune to himself! But clearly his diplomacy and charm had worked, because the next and all subsequent mornings, the lady of the house brought us a very welcome jug of hot sweet tea at about the time we were rousing ourselves for the day's tasks.

That night Bill O'Brien and I undertook the first of 17 operational PNG sorties. It was a relatively simple task of shifting an underslung load of supplies from the BMA in San Carlos Water to 45 Commando's new position at Teal Inlet. As far as we were concerned, it went splendidly well, and it gave us the confidence we needed to progress to the more challenging tasks that were to follow. Only much later did we find out that, due to our limited spatial awareness when using PNG, we had pinned the poor guy trying to hook up the underslung load between it and our undercarriage, nearly crushing him to death in the process!

It transpired that the same night, the Brigade Mountain and Arctic Warfare Cadre (who were operating in their war role of medium reconnaissance for the Brigade), located an Argentinean OP at Top Malo House and, in a bold assault the following morning, took it out. Other Argentinean OPs in the area, which had been tracking and reporting the Brigade's movement, fearing a similar fate, quickly gave themselves up. Quite apart from the wider good, it gave us aircrew some relief that the threat to helicopters from ground fire was now considerably reduced.

Up until this point, we had pretty much relied on the LPDs and RFAs, for fuel. However, as we became shore based and started to range further from the anchorage, from which RFAs were, in any case departing once unloaded, fuel started to become an issue. Fortunately, Larry Rotchell, had foreseen the need for Forward Arming and Refueling Points (FARP) which are designed, as the name suggests to support aircraft in the forward battle area. Larry organised two FARPs, as eloquently recorded by Sgt Brisbane in a 1982 edition of the REME Journal, 'The Craftsman':

In the beginning there was nothing and darkness was across the face of the Air Squadron and the E.M.E. (Larry) said "Let there be a FARP" and there was and the EME saw the FARP and saw that it was good. An evening and a morning brought D day -3 and, on this day, the EME went up to a great height and he saw the FARP was without shape or form. So, he gathered all the REME's that dwelt in the darkness within the depths of the Flights and put the REME's into the FARP whereupon they began to forage tools and bits of locking wire and SNEB test kits. The EME saw this and was pleased. Another evening and morning brought D-Day – 2, on this day the EME saw that the FARP was alone and pronounced "Let there be two species of FARP". There was a great rushing and dividing within the midst of the REME kit of the species of FARP. From this came FARP one and FARP two, the EME saw this and he saw it was good. An evening and a morning brought D-Day – 1, on this day EME saw the FARP's and he saw they were without knowledge and he said, "Let there be a briefing". The EME moved amongst the FARP's and they felt his breath upon their cheeks and much understanding brought a light to their eyes. An evening and a morn brought D-Day, the FARP's went forth into the foreign lands and on that day the EME rested.

FARP 1 deployed on D Day, in Ajax Bay, co-located with B Flight and close to the BMA; FARP 2 was later deployed to Port San Carlos.

When M Flight moved forward to our FOB at Teal Inlet, we were supplied with our own drum fuel and zenith pumps[23] to look after ourselves and avoid the need constantly to fly 46 km to San Carlos simply to refuel. This not only saved time but provided some welcome relief for the groundcrew; as Charlie Walker recalled, "Grabbing cabs to bring in fuel and take away empties got us into contact with the outside world a bit!" Monster's main role became re-fuelling:

Not only for M FLT, but later we had other flights using us, due to the fact they couldn't get on the flight decks of the ships. Or, as in the case of the Scouts, they were dropping off causalities, we were able to assist with getting the causalities from the pods on the side. re-fuel and turn them around quickly. I recall one of the cabs having a shrapnel hole in the neck of the fuel tank and the fuel pouring out when it was nearly full, we had to try and get the nozzle below the hole to re-fuel it.

As things progressed, FARP 1 relocated alongside us in Teal Inlet for a while, before moving on to Estancia House, again co-locating with B Flight. FARP 2 was eventually deployed to Fitzroy. Following the advance into Stanley, both FARP's were relocated to the Racecourse.

FARP 1 at Estancia House

---

[23] Zenith pumps are small electric pumps, powered by an aircraft's own battery with a pipe that inserts into the fuel drum and a hose with nozzle to deliver the fuel to the aircraft.

Fast and low beside a useful gully, in case of need

Meanwhile, 59 Squadron Royal Engineers had built a bulk fuel installation (BFI) at Port San Carlos, to be operated by the Commando Logistic Regiment, primarily to provide high pressure (HP) refueling for the larger SH and possibly Harriers. But it also had a low pressure (LP) outlet, for our smaller aircraft requiring 'open line[24]' refueling . A useful facility but not without hazard – as Bill O'Brien discovered:

I was sitting in the aircraft having a cigarette during a 'hot' refuel at the BFI, while Dolly was assisting the refueller. The nozzle release jammed, fuel started pouring down the side of the aircraft and it became pandemonium out there. The refueller had an epiphany and ran over to the LP outlet on the HP line, grabbed the hose and tore it out of the HP line. A geyser of HP fuel shot out and drenched the aircraft before they could shut down the HP line. There was a meaty engine surge and I quickly put my cigarette out. A quiet word with Charlie Walker later confirmed that the surge had not caused any damage!

On Tuesday, 1st June, the newly arrived 5 Brigade started to disembark in San Carlos Water, whilst the HQ of 3 Commando Brigade began to arrive at Teal Inlet. With 42 Commando, and 3 Para now established in the hills overlooking Stanley, the pace slowed a little, to allow 5 Brigade to disembark and move into position, and for artillery ammunition to be stockpiled on the gunlines in preparation for a final assault. However, another threat was emerging. The southern hemisphere winter was closing in fast and the weather had been deteriorating steadily since we landed. Long periods of fog, heavy snow, and fierce winds interspersed with short periods of dazzling sunshine became the norm. Conditions for the troops on the hills were appalling and flying conditions were often well below normal minima, making it hard for aircraft to reach unit locations.

With supply and communication lines becoming stretched, and a severe shortage of SH, the Squadron became mostly employed in a quasi-SH role. We began flying almost

---

[24]Open line refuelling is the way you fill a car, whereas HP requires the nozzle to be sealed and locked to the aircraft

continuously between San Carlos Water and the forward troops, shuffling people and supplies. The ground between was largely open and offered little protection. As Julian Thompson observed in his book 'No Picnic[25]', "it would surely be only a matter of time before the Argentine Air Force started to attack this vulnerable line of communication and supply". We flew fast and low, in tactical pairs as much as possible, keeping a watchful eye open for the threat, at the same time looking for folds in the ground where we might seek cover. After the experience of Goose Green, we feared the Pucara and some had formed the view that, if engaged, the best option might be simply to blast our Matra rockets in the general direction of any threat, then throw the aircraft on to the ground as quickly as possible and run away bravely!

However, when flying fast and low, enemy aircraft are not the only threat. Angus Horswill was flying as number two to Will Scott in loose formation, behind and some two hundred meters on Will's starboard side, both of them at very low level and maximum speed:

We had been briefed that on the Falklands the various settlements were connected to Stanley by a telephone network the cables for which were suspended on fence posts about a meter off the ground to allow sheep to pass underneath, but these were few and far between. Whenever a telephone line was spotted the lead aircraft would call "wire" on the radio as a heads up to the following aircraft. On this occasion Will called "wire" which ran at right angles to our track, which I spotted and overflew. As there was a creek bed heading my direction of travel, I descended, to make maximum use of the ground. Unknown to me between the position where Will crossed the wire and I did there was a branch line that went to the northwest but instead of being on fence posts it was just stretched across the creek bed. What followed was hair raising to say the least.

There was a sudden loud bang and the aircraft immediately pitched nose down, and rapidly decelerated, throwing me into my harness. To my horror, I saw a cable draped over the nose of the aircraft entangled in the VHF homing aerial. We were decelerating but still going fast; it was as if we were drawing some enormous bowstring with the aircraft as the arrow. The line eventually snapped but we were still in serious trouble. I was acutely aware that if the wire passed up and over the nose of the aircraft it would become entangled in the control rods for the main rotor which would then be crushed by the wire as it wound around them with the rotation of the rotor head. This would result in complete loss of control leading to a crash at high speed. I therefore had to flare the aircraft nose up as smoothly as possible to stop it riding up and land as quickly as possible. The line was now paying out across the nose of the aircraft and was now acting like a giant wire saw and starting to cut its way through the structure of the aircraft. I had no idea how much wire was left and as the ground in front was flat grass elected to do a high-speed running landing. We touched down at speed but I knew that I now had to lower the collective as gently as possible so as to gradually settle the weight of the aircraft on the skids, any sudden lowering of the collective would instantaneously transfer the entire weight onto the skids and possibly rip them off at the speed we were careering across the ground. At some stage before we came to a halt the end of the wire passed over the nose, flicked up, was hit by one of the retreating main rotor blades and accelerated to a speed with sufficient energy to slice off

25 Thompson (1985) p105

about a foot from the top of the tail fin. The cut was so clean that it was only noticed by the engineers later when they went to check the aircraft lights prior to night flying and found the anti-collision light missing along with a portion of the tail fin. When I finally stopped, I shut down and transmitted a Mayday call which fortunately the other aircraft heard. Yet again another change of underpants! With no washing facilities I was starting to run out of clean pairs!

Will and Ken recovered the crew of CM, leaving the damaged aircraft, where it had landed. As soon as I learned of this setback, I took John Hopkinson and Charlie Walker to inspect the damage and see what they could do to salvage CM. Luckily, the damage was limited to a broken ADF aerial, the canopy missing a sizeable piece of Perspex from the lower starboard (pilot) side, and a slice off the top of the starboard side stabiliser. In any other circumstances it would have been unflyable, which would have reduced M Flight to one serviceable aircraft. Fortunately, this was war and our LAD were both authorised and prepared for carrying out battle damage repair (BDR). Some head scratching, polythene sheeting and masking tape later, Hopkinson told me the aircraft was serviceable, for one flight only, back to the FOB. I asked if he was prepared to fly with me, which he readily agreed to do. That was all the assurance I needed, and we flew back to the FOB where the LAD set to work on a repair that would hopefully be a little more substantial.

With the temporary loss of CM, support to 45 Commando continued into the night, with Bill O'Brien and me flying the remaining serviceable aircraft, CZ, on PNG, to complete the days tasking. When we finally returned to the FOB, at around midnight, Peter Cameron was in the CP and announced that he had come to see how things were going with PNG. He wanted to fly to the Brigade HQ at San Carlos. I stood Bill down and prepared to fly with Peter. As we turned to leave the CP, Peter flipped his goggles down over his eyes and promptly walked into a doorpost, causing one of the most extreme outbursts of strangled mirth, from others in the room, that I have ever seen, not to mention a few 'Hail Marys'. The impact must have loosened the helmet bracket on which Peter's PNG were mounted because, almost as soon as we were airborne, he declared that he could not see anything. Following my earlier PNG 'check ride', I had discovered, a loose mounting bracket to be the cause my problems and I must confess to taking some perverse pleasure from taking control and flying fast and low, as Peter struggled to regain focus, thus letting him feel how it had been for me on the previous occasion!

I am aware that the narrative, thus far, has been almost totally focused on the activities of the aircrew which, I am ashamed to say, accurately reflects my obsession with flying operations at the time. But it was at about this point of the campaign that I started to properly appreciate the incredible contribution of the groundcrew, which was somehow enabling us to keep delivering with only 2 aircraft. The LAD was organised in two teams of four, each led by a Class 1 Sergeant, Ian Stuart, and Charlie Walker respectively; both were overseen by the ASM, John Hopkinson. Each team was supported by 3 of the aircraft handlers. They were nominally working defence watches of 8 hours on and 8 hours off but, much of the time, they just kept going until the job was done, particularly Howard Carter, who was the only Class 1 electrical engineer. In these expeditionary conditions, away from the usual support, as Charlie Walker put it, they "had to do a fair bit of swapping components between the two cabs to diagnose faults—torque meter and instrument systems in particular". Also, they taught the aircrew how to contribute to keeping the aircraft in the air. Charlie Walker recalls that shortly after advancing to Teal Inlet:

> One of the cabs developed an intermittent starting fault which meant having to short out a couple of pins in one of the ECU[26] pressure switches, using a small piece of locking wire. All the aircrew guys knew how to do this and carried a piece of wire in their overalls in case it happened away from REME support.

The care and ingenuity they showed to keep our aircraft available is best illustrated by the repair of CM. After further assessment, the LAD decided that it would be a good idea to replace one of CM's rotor head pitch change servos that had been struck by the telegraph wire. Unfortunately, there were none immediately available in the system and there was no other aircraft available for "cannibalisation" [27]... or was there? Somebody (I'm not sure who) suggested that we should check the wreckage of CY, still lying on the ground at Port San Carlos. A quick sortie later, we had the servo we needed and BDR on CM was underway! With everything else complete, over a very wet night at the FOB, Charlie Walker and Howard Carter, alternating between kneeling in a 4-inch puddle on the outside and the cramped but dry cockpit interior, stitched a thick fertilizer bag into the space of the missing Perspex. It took hours, drilling dozens of 1/16th' holes in the remaining Perspex but CM was back in service the on 2nd June, less than 48 hours after a serious accident, and the repairs were still in place at the end of the campaign, a fitting tribute to the initiative, skill and dedication of our small LAD team!

Whilst the technicians were doing their bit, the handlers assisted with aircraft husbandry, for example, the unpleasant task of cleaning cockpit interiors which we aircrew often brought home covered in blood, but which were miraculously clean the next time we flew.

With 3 Commando Brigade HQ now at Teal inlet, we were tasked to collect the, recently arrived, Divisional Commander, Jeremy Moore, to see the Commando Brigade situation for himself and discuss his intentions with Julian Thompson. Since Moore had previously taken me through officer training and been my CO when I was a Troop Commander in 42 Commando, I flew the sortie myself, to see what information I could glean from him during the transit. However, having been out of communication for ten days, he was too engrossed in his briefing papers, to make small talk with a 'gobby' pilot.

---

[26] ECU: Engine Control Unit
[27] Cannibalisation is common practice in under resourced aircraft fleets, where spares are short, and involves taking a part from an out of use aircraft to make another serviceable.

Sir Percival at Teal Inlet

The next day CM was back in action, but low cloud and fog began to set in and was to remain for the next few days. Sir Lancelot appeared in Teal Inlet that day, to offload a forward element of the BMA plus a forward dressing station. To our delight, she was soon followed by Sir Percival, who remained at anchor for several days. For us, this was manna from heaven and we quickly re-established our 'ships-flight' status. Under the pretext of using her for refueling, we started to scrounge some beer and fresh rations, most preciously, bread. We even managed to ferry people out to grab a shower. Once again Sir Percival was doing us proud, but not everybody benefited. Monster never got to the ship:

The weather took a turn for the worse and I recall being glad that I had invested in Norwegian shirts, and my good old faithful Nevisport Jacket (wax cotton) while serving in 45 Cdo. We didn't have the luxury of having a shower, I didn't get a shower from landing until ENDEX - wet Flannel and bucket of water only. I only had 2 pairs of underwear and limited clean dry clothes in my backpack. When opening a cab door to plug in the zenith pump on occasions you would get the smell of freshly showered aircrew. We must have stunk!!! But I knew they would be bedding down in the same barn, with an unwashed sleeping bag at the end of the day.

We tried our best to share the good fortune. Angus recalls that JC came up with the idea that:

every time anyone landed on a ship to refuel, our observers would make a bee line straight for the ships galley, in order to scrounge whatever they could get hold of in the way of rations be it raw veg or tinned goods. Then when we landed at a forward location, we would hand it out to any marine we came across.

During this period, the days and nights seemed to roll together. 45 Commando moved forward to Bluff Cove Peak and joined the patrolling already being conducted by 42 Commando and 3 Para. We heard that, at the same time, 2 Para had made a bold move to fly into Bluff Cove, on the other side of the mountains. Tasking became routine, albeit challenging, due to the low cloud and fog. Bill Obrien recorded that:

We continued to move kit and stores left behind in the long yomp. Some troops had been without the comfort of even a sleeping bag since they started. We all knew how they felt, so went the extra mile in the worsening weather, following fence lines and in some cases putting crewmen out in front on foot to lead the aircraft through the more difficult patches.

With no PNG possible in the poor weather conditions, I took the opportunity to placate the other aircrew by making Bill do a couple of stints as duty pilot. Chafing at his grounding, Bill learned new skills from the handlers, such as brewing 'wets' with plastic explosive (PE)!

The PE burned so hot that water boiled in a couple of seconds, but the real secret of success was to light it only with ordinary matches and NEVER anything with piezoelectric ignition, lest you brewed up a great deal more than just a wet[28]!

With bad weather continuing, it finally became necessary for somebody to reach 42 Commando on the top of Mount Kent, whatever the risk, because their crypto[29] was about to expire and, somehow, the task fell to M Flight. The weather was way out of all known limits, so I elected to fly the sortie myself with Dolly Drummond as crew. The flight to the foot of the mountain, below the main cloud, was straightforward but, we then began to ascend up a short, steep re-entrant into ever thickening cloud, in order to reach a bowl just beyond Bluff Cove Peak, where 42 Commando's HQ and Support Company were based. With visibility down to feet, we adapted a 'whiteout' technique, learned in Norway, of fixing on nearby ground reference points then hover taxiing from one point of reference to the next, until eventually we were in the bowl. However, it was huge – at least a square kilometre - visibility was strictly limited and we did not have 42's exact positions. Phil Wilson (OC Support Company) was on the radio trying to direct us towards himself but, with only the sound of our aircraft, bouncing off every side of the bowl, to indicate our position, was having no success. Finally, in frustration, he radioed, "stay where you are, I'll come to you", which he did and, rather in the manner of early automobiles, we meekly taxied after him as he walked us back to his company position. Even from our cosy aircraft cockpit, the privations of their location were clear, ponchos

---

[28] Wet: Many uses. In this case a mug of tea (Jolly 1999 p499).
[29] Crypto was the term for the data to be input to radios to allow secure communication and needed regular updating.

stretched over rocks under which marines were huddled, seeking meagre shelter from the pervading wetness.

Having delivered the crypto and as many ration packs as we had been able to squeeze into the back of the aircraft, we were about to depart when Phil came forward and asked us to evacuate Pat Bishop – an accredited war correspondent - who was failing to cope with the appalling conditions on Mount Kent. As they led him to the aircraft, I could see that he looked close to death, drawn and grey; his very soul seemed to be wet and cold and, clearly, he had nothing left in reserve. With Pat safely (so he thought) curled up on the back seat, Phil led us back to the top of the re-entrant that was our route home and waved us goodbye. But the drama was not yet over. When hover taxiing up a mountain, the aircraft tail points away from the slope but, going down, … enough said! When I tried to fly a bit higher, to allow for the tail sticking out behind, I lost ground reference so, we taxied backwards down the re-entrant, with Dolly hanging out of the door and directing me, until we finally broke cloud and could return to normal service.

On another occasion, flying with JC, we were seeking to find 3 Para on Mount Vernon. Once again visibility was so bad that the ground immediately below was the only external reference available to us. At one point, I unexpectedly found myself over water with no ground reference. Instrument flying at 20 feet with potential obstacles all round is not to be recommended! After what felt like an age but was probably no more than a few seconds, I picked up a fresh reference point and we continued to grope our way forward. I cannot remember if we found the Paras or not but do recall that, at one point, we became convinced that we had overflown our own front line and were close to that of the enemy. We lost no time in reversing our track!

I was not just the troops who were suffering from the appalling weather. The settlement manger had approached Andrew Eames and asked him to move us out of our cosy barn because his animals were suffering, and he needed to get them into shelter. Fortunately for us, Andrew refused to do so until alternative accommodation could be found. As other units moved forward, more space became available at Teal Inlet and we were able to move to a corrugated iron walled, concrete floored machinery store with a separate room for our CP. It was not as warm as our hay filled barn, but it had electric lighting and you could smoke without having to brave the, usually wet and cold, elements.

On 4th June, we were directed to take CZ to the newly arrived Air Maintenance Group (AMG)[30] back in San Carlos for a routine head change. Given the stresses that we had routinely been applying to the transmission systems of all the aircraft, this order, applying peacetime rules - which temporarily reduced the flight to one aircraft at such a busy time - seemed ironic at best, ludicrous at worst. Having been absent during the crucial refits at Ascension Island, where they could have added real value, it seemed to me, perhaps unfairly, that the AMG were now trying to justify their belated presence.

---

[30] An AMG is a REME organisation, designed to deliver major routine servicing requirements for equipment that are beyond the scope of the capacity or skills of a units integral LAD.

Will Scott enjoying our new accommodation

With my flight reduced to one damaged aircraft, I pleaded for the return of CK but was told to get back in my box.

By 6th June, the visibility had improved somewhat, and PNG sorties were again required. That night, with Bill O'Brien flying and me navigating, we set out to CASEVAC a Marine Patterson of 42 Commando from close to Mt Harriet, where he had stepped on a mine during a patrol. Because of cloud over the high ground, we decided to go the long way, round the mountains, via San Carlos Water, and to cross the front through 2 Para's lines at Fitzroy. With no radio contact and not wishing to be shot down as an Argentinian intruder on the way back (given earlier reports of 2 Para engaging an A Flight Gazelle on Sussex Mountain) we decided to land and make physical contact before crossing their front line. Unsurprisingly, with no specific grid reference, the Paras position was hard to find in the dark, even with our wonderful PNG. Desperate to contact the Paras but also keen to press on, I told Bill to land by a farmhouse that we had seen, and I ran over to knock on the door. To my surprise, the lady who opened the door screamed, and almost went into shock. When I think back on it, I should not have been surprised. In bulky flying clothing and flying helmets, we already looked like alien beings, made infinitely spookier in the dark by the downward green glow from the PNG when they were turned up, away from the eyes. To make things worse, as I was running towards the house, I had stumbled and the goggles had snapped down, cutting the bridge of my nose, which had begun to bleed profusely, without me realising it. It was clearly not a pretty site that greeted her! Having regained her composure, she said that she had not seen any British troops in the area, so we decided to push on and take our chances on return, reckoning that if we used this same route on the way back we would not encounter 2 Para.

The pick-up was close to Argentinean positions on Mount Harriet and believed to be in a minefield, so we proceeded with some trepidation. As we approached to land, Bill saw vehicle tracks, showing clearly in the snow and, on the assumption that there would be no mines where there were tracks, he set down on these. Patterson was quickly lifted into the back of the aircraft and, retracing our route, we had soon delivered him to the dressing station in Ajax Bay.

We learned later that on the same night, a Gazelle from 656 Sqn was shot down by HMS Cardiff, in a 'blue on blue' engagement, whilst the aircraft was conducting a resupply sortie to a radio rebroadcast site high on Pleasant Peak. The ship had been moved, to interdict Argentinean air attacks. 5 Brigade was unaware of the ship's presence and the ship unaware of the aircraft's task. To compound this, aircraft were flying with IFF[31] switched off, apparently because it interfered with the Rapier air defence system. Bill and I thanked our lucky stars that the weather had stopped us crossing over the mountains, or that might have been us.

The 8th of June was unusually clear and bright. Having delivered them some stores, 42 Commando asked us to fly a laser target marker (LTM) to an artillery forward observer team on Wall Mountain which is, in effect, a forward spur of Mount Challenger, about 2 kms from Mount Harriet and Two Sisters, where the Argentineans had strong defensive positions. I protested that this would mean flying down the forward slope of Mount Challenger for about 3 kms in full view of the enemy. Whoever was on the radio was initially quite scathing about my lack of 'bottle', until I pointed out that we would probably be in and out before the enemy could react but that we would have clearly pinpointed the presence of the observer team. After a short pause, the unit operations officer, Ian McNeill, took over the conversation and said that they understood the risk to both us and their observer team but, in their considered judgement, the need to get the LTM forward outweighed these risks. I knew Ian well, we had served together a few years earlier in Dhofar, on loan to the Sultan of Oman's Army; he had been the best man at my wedding and was to be a godfather to my, as yet unseen, new-born son. I knew he was a consummate professional so, took him at his word and said we would give it a try. We collected the LTM and operator from 7 Battery then, at full tilt, crossed over the saddle between Mount Kent and Mount Challenger, contouring around the forward slope, into safety behind the crest of Wall Mountain where we unceremoniously dropped off the LTM and its operator, before quickly making the open dash back over the saddle. As we had hoped, it was all too quickly for the enemy to engage us, but I never heard what problems it caused subsequently for the observer team.

---

[31] Identification Friend or Foe is a device fitted to aircraft that emits a coded signal that should identify it to friendly forces.

Angus Horswill was later asked to fly a similar task:

... which entailed flying to the south side of Mount Kent and landing. I can't remember if it was a passenger pick up or drop but I remember being briefed that the position was in view of enemy observation but out of range of any direct fire weapons and probably artillery and mortars as well. Once we'd done whatever we had to, we flew westwards and had a panoramic view of the whole south side of the Island with unlimited visibility. What should I see to my horror but two LSLs anchored in the vicinity of Fitzroy. I knew immediately that if we could see them they were definitely in plain view of Argentinean observers. I'm sure that I passed this info on but at that stage it was far too late and was overtaken by events.

What Angus had seen at Fitzroy, was the RFAs Sir Galahad and Sir Tristram unloading the Welsh Guards, who they had ferried from San Carlos. In the afternoon, came the now well-known attack by two Mirages and two Skyhawks, which resulted in the loss of Sir Galahad and the deaths of 51 sailors and soldiers with a further 46 injured, together with the loss of untold personal equipment and clothing by many more. A later attack was driven off from Fitzroy but chanced upon and sank an LCM making its slow way from Goose Green, loaded with vital radio vehicles for 5 Brigade HQ.

That same day, CZ was returned from the AMG but still required work to be completed by our own LAD. The next day I flew CZ solo, to conduct an air test and then take General Moore and some of his staff forward, firstly to inspect the carnage at Fitzroy and then to meet my own Brigade Commander. En-route to San Carlos, to pick up Moore, I had a serious scare when a Sea Harrier broke through the cloud base, clearly locked onto me and ready to attack. Fortunately, the pilot's visual recognition was good, and he pulled up, just as I had started a forlorn evasive break. With Moore and two of his staff on board, we flew straight to Fitzroy, where a sobering sight greeted us. The ships were still burning and a black pall of smoke hung over the inlet, whilst helicopters and landing craft milled around them, braving the fire and risk of explosions, as they continued to rescue those still aboard and recover what stores and equipment they could. Whilst Moore and his staff were being briefed on the situation, I sought out the aviation cell in 5 Brigade HQ, hoping to get intelligence and radio frequencies for their area. However, with the mishaps of the last 24 hours and loss of its CP vehicles on the sunk LCM, the cell was struggling to pull together any coherent information and were unable to provide help. Once Moore had completed his assessment of the situation, I flew him and his staff to Estancia House, to meet with Thompson and review plans for the next phase.

As 5 Brigade regathered itself, our own Brigade was obliged to pause. For M Flight, life at Teal Inlet became quieter for a few days. However, following the dreadful event at Fitzroy, the Chinese crewmen refused to stay on board in daylight, whilst the LSLs were at anchor in Teal Inlet. So, they were ferried ashore at first light and would sit all day in a corrugated iron shearing shed, in their anti-flash gear and tin helmets, shivering in the wet and cold conditions, before being returned to the ships at last light. During one air raid warning, some mischievous soul - not a member of M Flight I hasten to add

- threw a load of rocks onto the roof of the shed which rattled noisily over the corrugated iron, creating a panic and scattering the Chinese crewmen across the settlement!

The scene was now being set for the final act of our drama.

The Area Round Stanley

End Game: The Taking of Stanley

On the 10th June, Thompson held his O Group, for what he later titled the "Night Battle[32]", to capture the ring of hills immediately surrounding Stanley and set the conditions for a final assault. There were to be three simultaneous attacks on Mounts Harriet, Two Sisters and Longdon by 42 Commando, 45 Commando and 3 Para respectively, starting during the night of 11th June. 2 Para had been re-assigned to the Commando Brigade, with the task of providing a reserve for this stage of the battle but ready to exploit success and push on to seize Wireless Ridge, if things went well. I flew to Fitzroy to collect their new CO, David Chandler, who had, literally, been parachuted in to replace 'H' Jones. I told him that we had been in direct support of 2 Para at Goose Green and that it was good to see them back with our Brigade, to which I received a vehement response that they too were glad to be back; make of that what you will. As the Squadron contribution to the forthcoming battle, M Flight was placed in direct support of 45 Commando, with A Flight to 42 Commando and C Flight to 3 Para; B Flight was to be the Brigade Reserve.

After the orders, COs had to get back to their units but the weather in the mountains had, once again, deteriorated. Terry Waldron was tasked to fly the CO of 45 Commando back to his CP at Bluff Cove Peak;

The best I could do was hover taxi up the side of the mountain in search of the CP. After about 10 minutes, no marines could be found. However, the CO was sure we had the correct area and suggested that he continue on foot. We agreed that I would wait for 10 minutes. If he didn't return, I should assume he had found the CP. I managed to land on several large boulders without tipping the aircraft over and the CO went on his way. With my door open and a cigarette in hand I watched the minutes tick by. Suddenly, I felt a tap on my leg. Looking down, I saw a face covered in cam cream, smiling up at me and holding up a black mug of tea. There was a section camped out under and around the boulders that I had landed on! I returned the cup, together with a packet of cigarettes and went on my way.

The weather problem was not confined only to getting COs back to their units. The Brigade HQ was unable to transmit the artillery fire plan for the attack to the batteries up on Mount Kent so, it had to go by courier. Will Scott and Ken Priest picked up a staff officer armed with the plan and, once again in thick fog, hover taxied up the mountain, finally, encountering the gun batteries as they loomed out of the fog. The plans

---

[32] Thompson (1985) Ch 9

were safely delivered - saving the day, we liked to think - certainly the artillery staff officer seemed very relieved.

That night, as the Brigade continued to patrol aggressively, to probe Argentinian positions and keep them unsettled, two of the patrols sent out from 45 Commando met unexpectedly. One was from Support Company, Mortar Troop and the other from one of the rifle companies. There had clearly been some problem with the patrol matrix; neither patrol knew the other was in the area and they ended up in a furious firefight. Bill and I, already airborne on another PNG task, were redirected to evacuate the casualties. On this occasion, I was flying, and Bill was navigating. We were given little detail of the task, except a location from which to collect casualties so, when we landed, Bill got out to see what was wanted and soon discovered that the situation was grim:

When we arrived on scene there was a young navy medic, clearly in shock himself, in the back of a BV, with 3 very seriously injured casualties. As I opened the door, he showed me the serious wounds to the back of one of the casualties and said, "what should I do?" "How the f*** should I know", I said, "I'm a pilot not a f***ing doctor. Get them into the bloody helicopter!". It was not what he wanted to hear, and it was not my finest moment, but I really didn't know what else to say.

On the morning of 11th June, I attended 45 Commando's 'O' Group and agreed to provide a LO to their HQ for the duration of the battle. I nominated Will Scott for the job; he said afterwards, he knew it was coming his way, clearly the Flight Commander was not going to do it and he was the only other officer in the flight. Will spent the day trying to gather appropriate infantry equipment for the task, in particular a combat helmet and a rifle. As aircrew, all we had were pistols and flying helmets. It was no good going to the Squadron Quartermaster, we had long become used to the stock answer for any stores request, "sorry those are on the [MV] Elk", a container ship on which the Squadron B Echelon had travelled South but from which it had not managed to successfully unload much stock. In fact, it had become a standard joke that anything missing or unavailable was "on the Elk". Will implored Ian Mellor, the flight sergeant, to lend him his combat helmet and rifle, as he was going to the front line. At first Mellor refused but, after much argument, relented a little and offered his helmet, for which he made Will sign, but he would not give up his SLR.

Towards evening, Will Scott together with a signaller, Will Parker, was flown forward, to join 45 Commando at their position on Bluff Cove Peak. However, the CO had decided to move early, to an assembly area just north of Mount Kent, at Murrel Bridge, to reduce the distance to be covered in darkness to the start line for the attack. Only a small security detail was left at the unit's base position. A sensible move but, unfortunately, no one told us. Will takes up the story:

We had no option but to move forward on foot, in broad daylight, with no more than the directions of two Marines who were still in the area. Armed with only one 9mm pistol and an SMG between us and carrying a UHF radio (that was useless for talking to ground troops) we set off down the forward slope of Mount Kent, to try and catch up with 45 Commando. It wasn't long before we attracted the attention of Argentine artillery observers and, whilst we laboriously clambered down the *slippery rocky surface, artillery shells started landing around us. Fortunately, the rocks offered reasonable cover and soon it got dark. Eventually, we made it to a track that we had been assured was clear of landmines and started to make quicker progress. Unbeknown to us, at the time, we were now some half a mile forward of 45 Commando's Mortar Troop, who had repositioned the night before, and who now decided to 'bed in' their mortars with a few rounds per tube. The area lit up with unexpected muzzle flashes of mortar charges going off and, a few moments later, we clearly saw the mortar rounds impacting the Two Sister's feature, the intended target of 45 Commando's assault. This at least gave us reassurance about where we were but at the same time, we realised that we were now in front of 45 Commando's rear elements, so going back was not really an option, as we would most likely be mistaken for enemy. The inevitable return fire was not long in coming. Distant muzzle flashes of artillery fire, from behind the Two Sisters feature, were unmistakable and we threw ourselves into a bog for cover. Fortunately, the Argentine fire was random and inaccurate, shells whooshed over and impacted around the area but to no real affect. Will Parker's pack was hit by some fizzing shrapnel and, once an interlude came, I had to pull him out of the bog, to carry on. My combat helmet, so hard worked for and signed for, had fallen off and rolled away into the grass, never to be seen again! We progressed nervously forward, very aware that we were in 'no man's land' and at considerable risk of being seen as 'enemy' by both sides. At last, we encountered a friendly patrol that had been sent along the track to find us. At the first sound ahead we froze, then heard a classic challenge of 'Who goes there'. Relieved to hear a British voice, I called out my rank and name, the response was "where the f*** have you been?". We were led to safety and then got ready for our role in the coming assault.*

Whilst this small drama was playing out, I gave Bill O'Brien and Dolly Drummond a task to fly urgent press dispatches back to HMS Fearless in San Carlos Water, the only ship that had the necessary strategic communication to relay them back to UK. It was a calm, bright night, so Bill let Dolly have the controls, while he read through the press reports. One was a graphic, blow by blow account of the attack on Two Sisters; but this was hours before 45 Commando had even crossed the start line for the assault to begin. Indignant and angry they ditched the report in San Carlos Water, before landing on HMS Fearless, to hand over the remainder. We wondered afterwards, which journalist was left wondering why he never got the 'scoop', that he had scurrilously hoped for.

The three-pronged assault by 3 Commando Brigade got underway a few hours after darkness fell and, as the night wore on, seemed to be going well[33], except on Mount Longdon, where 3 Para were engaged in a fierce battle against a strong Argentinean force and taking a lot of casualties. Bill and I were still, the only PNG qualified crew in the Squadron so, were sent to support to 3 Para – the direct support task for 45 Commando was only due to commence "from dawn". We spent about two hours shuttling between the 3 Para regimental aid post, on the western slopes of Longdon, and the forward dressing station, now located at Estancia House. I cannot remember how many trips we did, but there were a lot of casualties to be moved.

---

[33] The final casualty figures for this battle were 23 dead and 43 wounded.

We came off task shortly before dawn, to allow direct support for 45 Commando to commence, in accordance with the Brigade plan. 45 Commando's battle had been successful, and M Flight was now busy helping them to consolidate on Two Sisters and evacuate their wounded. Given that we were being used to support other units as well, I wanted to speak with the CO to have the best possible idea of his needs and ensure that these would somehow be met. I also wanted to facilitate the relief of Will Scott by Terry Waldron as the aviation LO. So, having breakfasted and shaved, I hitched a lift to Mount Harriet. I saw Andrew Whitehead standing near the summit, with his Operations Officer, Mike Hitchcock. Unsurprisingly, both were looking tired and grey after the events of a long hard night. I remember bouncing up to Whitehead, giving him my snappiest aircrew salute and wishing him good morning, which drew a thin smile and the response, "as long as you don't smell of aftershave, you might just get away with this"! Having established Andrew's priorities, I was flown back to our FOB with Will Scott, leaving Terry Waldron to carry on as the aviation LO.

Terry immediately came into the firing line,

45 were still in the process of reorganizing on Two Sisters. The CO personally, asked me to arrange a helicopter, to move their bergens/heavy equipment up to the troops at the top. I started to explain that it may take some time: HELQUEST[34] required, radio calls and all the normal procedures would slow things down. I remember the CO looking at me and saying, "don't give me your problems just get me a helicopter" and disappeared back inside the CP. Just then, a Seaking flew past and I quickly got on the UHF chat frequency and called the aircraft to quick stop and do a 180 - I had seen the call sign on the back of the aircraft. To my surprise, the Seaking did stop and turned 180. I stuck my hand in the air and said, "can you see me", they could. I pointed to the huge pile of bergens sitting next to the CP and asked if he could move the equipment up to the top. The boys up there wanted their breakfast. The CO came out of his CP to see what all the noise was about. "That's the helicopter you requested sir". He started to say something but probably thought better not to ask, turned around and went back into his CP. Less than 60 seconds from request to arrival of air support. Must have been a record!

The Flight remained busy all day, helping 45 to consolidate on Two Sisters. I flew some sorties with Ken Priest, ferrying supplies and battle casualty replacements (BCRs) from the Unit's A Echelon at Estancia House to the front line. Two memories stick in my mind. The first was the macabre situation of offloading two body bags at the same time as two BCRs were approaching the aircraft to be flown forward; I am sure that could have been better managed. The other was a surprising shortage of underslung cargo nets across the Brigade, until it was discovered that the QM of 3 Para was hoarding them back at Teal Inlet. We soon rectified that!

---

[34] A HELQUEST was the radio format used to request helicopter tasking

Evacuating a casualty from Two Sisters

The weather remained fine and clear, but the planned follow up assault on Mount Tumbledown by 5 Brigade was delayed by 24 hours and, with it, 2 Para's attack on Wireless Ridge. Through 13th June, we continued to assist the refurbishment of 45 Commando, shuttling between Two Sisters and their A Echelon, which was in the Forward BMA, close to Estancia House, where the Brigade HQ and the Squadron HQ were located. Bill O'Brien was there as slip crew and digging a trench, a procedure now ingrained in all of us, as protection against the possibility of air attack, helped by 2 marines from 45 Commando.

I didn't expect to be fighting from it, well obviously it was for aircrew, so it was much longer and deeper than a standard fire trench! Suddenly came the alarm - 'Air Raid Warning Red'. I jumped into the trench and was joined by Rodney Helme just before a few bombs fell. After only a few minutes came the 'all clear' and Rodney asked, 'Have you seen the Senior Pilot Sergeant O'Brien?'. I told him no. but heard later that Andrew Eames, still in a vest and with his face half covered in shaving cream, having been caught mid-ablution by the raid, appeared in front of a group of very anxious journalists, who had been waiting for a flight, and calmly announced, 'That was a close shave chaps!'

JC and I had a different perspective of this attack. We were flying west, towards Two Sisters, along the valley that lay between Mounts Kent and Estancia, when, to our horror, we saw 4 Skyhawks at low level coming the other way. I immediately broke left into a re-entrant on the southern side of Mount Estancia, which gave us some ground cover, then spun the aircraft though 180°, to point our rockets towards the threat, just in time to see them dropping bombs apparently bombing 3 Commando Brigade HQ. They then circled round, seemingly for another attack run; a red mist of unreasoning rage descended on me; how dare they! I was saying we would show them they couldn't get away with that sort of behaviour and instructing JC to go through the rocket arming sequence' which he dutifully did but at the same time managing to calm me down. He suggested that the best we would probably achieve would be no more than to annoy them and pointed out decisively that the Brigade HQ would be in the likely impact zone, when the rockets, inevitably, missed their intended targets!

We learned later that the Brigade HQ, the intended target, had been saved when the Argentinean pilots were diverted in their action at the last minute by targeting instead some aircraft parked on an LS, a short distance to the west of the HQ! Whilst the HQ was spared, it seems that we came close to losing both our Brigade Commander and our Squadron Commander who, about to fly to San Carlos Water, were approaching one of the parked Scout aircraft when the alarm went up. Several aircraft were damaged but, miraculously, there were no serious human casualties.

That night, the second wave of coordinated attacks was underway, this time 2 Para pushing on to Wireless Ridge, whilst the Scots Guards assaulted Mount Tumbledown. Our Squadron was supporting the Paras whilst 656 Sqn AAC supported the Guards. C Flight had now fielded a PNG crew, who were also in support of 2 Para, but it was still a busy night for Bill and I, ferrying ammunition forward and casualties

Brigade HQ LS at Estancia House

back, the same as Goose Green but in the dark. It was a long and eventful night and my memory of it consists of no more than a series of disconnected cameos. A real peril was the mixture of PNG and conventional night flying around the rear areas and, early on, after an extremely close encounter with a Wessex, we learned to 'light up' when out of the forward area.

A troop of Scimitars from the Blues and Royals was giving fire support to 2 Para, with their four vehicles 'hull down[35]' along a ridge overlooking the battlefield. We were dropping a second load of 'ammunition' just to the rear of their firing line, when a figure approached, clearly wanting to communicate. It was the troop commander, who very politely thanked us for our support but said they did not really need 'KIP[36]s' and would be incredibly grateful if we instead brought them the ammunition they had originally asked for! Unbeknown to us, 2 Para had requested 600 KIPs to flown to them before dawn, as they were concerned by their exposed position on top the ridge, and the C Flt PNG crew had been given this task. With hindsight, it seems that whoever was controlling the loading at the 2 Para Echelon was not aware that there were two Gazelles on different tasks. Another classic example of the "fog of war"! Having sorted out the confusion and certain that we had the required ammunition, we flew our next sortie to the Blues and Royals on Wireless Ridge but were now surprised when a Scout helicopter from B Flight, flown by WO2 'Robbie' Robinson (not PNG equipped) landed beside us. He explained later that he, had been tasked also for the ammunition resupply and seeing us being loaded with same, decided to tail us from Estancia House hoping that a) we knew what we were doing and b) he could keep us in sight. An incredibly brave man on both counts!

One particularly challenging, short notice task was to find and evacuate a seriously wounded casualty from D Squadron SAS. One of their patrols had run into trouble during a waterborne raid against a fuel depot on the north arm of Stanley harbour, intended to divert attention from 2 Para's attack on Wireless Ridge. They had been spotted and illuminated by the searchlights of an Argentine ship moored in Port William and engaged by anti-aircraft guns that were being used in an anti-boat role. Now safely ashore, they had taken up position north of Hearnden Water and several kilometres east of 2 Para, where there were believed still to be a few enemy positions. During the long night, Bill and I were switching roles regularly, to try and stay fresh; on this occasion, I was flying, whilst Bill had the navigation. We crept forward, as carefully as we could, to the given pick-up location, constantly alert for any sign of enemy activity. The grid was spot on and we soon found a huddle of SAS soldiers tending their casualties, whilst continuing to put down suppressive mortar fire on an enemy position to their north, on Twelve O'Clock Mountain. The casualty, Brummie Stokes, had been shot in the thigh and was in bad shape; the priority was to get him to the FDS, as quickly as possible. He

---

[35] 'Hull down' describes a profile where a vehicle is positioned behind cover with only its vision, sighting and, if necessary, weapon system exposed to enemy view.
[36] KIP: Individual Protection Kit (but commonly abbreviated in speech to KIP) used to help provide overhead cover for slit trenches.

was unceremoniously bundled into the back of the aircraft and we took off, pleased to be leaving such a dangerous area. However, the process of loading must have dislodged the tourniquet that had been put on him, because, as blood started pumping over us, it became clear that an arterial bleed had restarted. Whilst I focused on flying to the dressing station as quickly as possible, Bill leant into the rear of the cabin and did what he could to reduce the bleed. I am happy to say we got Brummie to the dressing station alive and learned later that he had survived.

During our final sortie that night, as 2 Para pushed further east and forward on Wireless Ridge, in the final phase of their attack, we suddenly found ourselves barely a kilometre from Stanley, with only the water of the harbour between us and the main Argentine forces. Tracer was flying around from every point of the compass, so, we quickly turned tail and withdrew behind the cover of the ridge. After 6½ hours of flying that night, Bill and I arrived back at Teal Inlet, just as dawn was breaking, and, exhausted, went straight to bed whilst the rest of the flight got on with the day job. Will Scott and Ken Priest took the Brigade Commander and the Gunner CO up to Wireless Ridge, to assess the situation. They shut down and watched, with the Brigade Staff, as the Argentineans streamed from their mountain positions, back into Port Stanley. Thompson was anxious lest they should seek to defend the town, which would require us to fight through the built-up areas. More to the point the Artillery Commander was pointing out

Argentinean Troops surrendering on Wireless Ridge

Will Scott's first view of Stanley

that he had only two rounds per gun left! It was a close-run thing, but it was obvious the Argentineans had had enough.

The Brigadier and Gunner CO returned to the Brigade HQ, as preparations were made for the surrender. Leading elements of 2 Para had already reached the edges of Stanley and with them was Max Hastings as an embedded reporter. Will Scott and Ken Priest were sent back to find him as it was deemed important that he file his report to the media as soon as possible. Unsure where to go and how far our troops had penetrated into Port Stanley, and certainly with no knowledge of possible mined areas, Will landed on the road near Government House, and asked some Para's who were there, to fetch Max Hastings. He eventually appeared and wrote his press copy in the back of the aircraft as they flew him to HMS Fearless back in San Carlos Water, where he could file his report.

I was woken up several hours later, on a bright cold morning, to be told that the Argentineans were surrendering. Strangely, I felt both relieved and deflated all at once, M Flight had come through the conflict without loss but the focus of my being for the last few months was suddenly gone. Bill O'Brien was woken by Ken Priest with a 'wet', "which smelt suspiciously like there was as much alcohol as coffee in it", and the news that the Argentineans had surrendered. Bill remembers that it was the first time in the campaign he became angry, "How dare they surrender when I was asleep and anyway, now what am I going to do tonight!".

The fighting was over, but much work still needed to be done. M Flight was again placed in direct support of 45 Commando, as it advanced into Stanley. JC and I were conducting a recce of the racecourse, as a potential HLS. We came to a hover near the stadium and started to rotate, to get a good look at what was there. What we were not expecting to see was a score or more of Argentinian troops emerging from hiding, trying to surrender to us! Since they appeared still to be armed, we decided on discretion and beat a hasty exit, informing 45 Commando of the Argentinean presence.

As more and more elements of 3 Commando Brigade advanced into Stanley, Will Scott and Ken Priest were tasked to go to Government House and provide an air taxi service for any staff that needed it, which gave them the chance for a short wander about Stanley and see for themselves the liberation of Stanley. It really was all over bar the shouting

Aftermath: Tidying Up and Cruising Home

With victory secured, Teal Inlet quickly emptied, as a rush for the bright lights of Stanley gathered momentum. However, given the mobility that we enjoyed, two things led us to decide to stay where we were. Firstly, soon after the ceasefire, the locals fed us a dinner of roast lamb, the first fresh meat most of us had eaten since landing, and we looked forward to more. Secondly, we found that we could now move into a bunkhouse with heating and hot water, purpose built for visiting sheep shearers and recently vacated by 3 Para, the like of which was unlikely to be available in an increasingly overcrowded Stanley.

For the next week, liaison flying (effectively air taxiing) was the norm, as the Brigade regrouped and reorganised. Will Scott and Ken Priest ferried the Brigade Major, John Chester, to Fox Bay on West Falkland, where 40 Commando were busy establishing control and taking droves of prisoners.

It was so strange to climb to a moderate altitude of perhaps 1000 feet; no one had flown much above 100 feet for several weeks. There was a surreal feel to life, suddenly the threats had gone and the whole resolve of our existence for the last 2 months had evaporated; life seemed rather purposeless, not joyful at all. Perhaps a moment of quiet reflection was needed to fill that empty, adrenaline filled space?

Similar tasks followed, Will and Ken next took a Red Cross Inspector to Goose Green, to review an accident that had occurred shortly after the battle there. Apparently, some Argentinean technicians had been asked to help deal with their unstable napalm bombs, which were still there. It seemed that one had ignited, engulfing one Argentinean technician in fire. For Will, the encounter with the inspector was an eye opener. She explained that, whilst it is a breach of the Geneva Convention to ask POW's to work, these were Argentinean munitions and, under the circumstances, it was their responsibility to make them safe. What had subsequently happened, the inspector regarded as a misadventure of war.

Captain Rod Boswell, commander of the Mountain and Arctic Warfare Cadre, was keen to return to Top Malo House, the scene of their spectacular action to take out an Argentinean OP. Will and Ken flew Rod there, keeping a close eye on him, as he was reported to be second only to the Argentineans in damaging the Squadron's aircraft, poking a rifle muzzle through the skin of one and breaking the door of another! But, as recompense, they got a personal battlefield tour from him.

JC and I flew a sortie to take the unit photographer from 2 Para to make a video of Goose Green. Waiting to pick him up in Stanley, I was standing next to the battle-scarred CM, when a young, local boy approached me and, with wide eyed respect, asked if the damage was from anti-aircraft fire or a dog fight. I told him no, it had hit some wires, whereupon the look of respect turned, instantly to scorn, as he pronounced, "you're not very good, are you?". Useless to try and explain that I had not been flying it at the time; I just had to take it on the chin, as my comeuppance for not having a decent war story up my sleeve!

Meanwhile, out at Teal Inlet, we were hearing tales of the food and cigarettes being "liberated" from Argentinean supplies by units that had entered Stanley. Having been living almost continuously on the same menu of arctic rations since landing, I was determined that M Flight should not miss out so, I tasked, Ian Mellor, together with Monster, to go to Stanley and "proff" as much of the available goodies as they could. Monster takes up the story:

Ian and I were dropped off with an under slung net on the outskirts of Stanley. Ian being a smoker and cigarettes being in short supply, his priority was to find cigarettes. Walking down the main drag there were shipping containers on the right hand side of the road with mine tape round them; on the left was the shoreline with mine tape all the way along, where the Argies had thought we would land. There were Marines rummaging through the containers and they assured us that as long as we stayed on the path to the containers, we would be fine, the mines were on the beach. They had found the Argentinean Officers ration packs which each contained a miniature of brandy, but no cigarettes! Ian pulled rank and pointed out that he needed nicotine. We continued until coming across another container, which had colour TV boxes in it, but happily, they were full of cigarettes and not TV's - one happy sergeant. I ended up drawing the short straw, as Ian offered to carry my SLR while I went to retrieve a box. We returned along the shore to the drop off point, Ian with two SLR's and me carrying a large TV box on my shoulders. This was the first box in the net. Ian then remained on guard with the booty while I went on a forage returning with boxes of tinned corned beef and a few other goodies.

Terry Waldron and JC went to pick up the Flight's 'hunter gatherers' and "were surprised to see an underslung net full of God knows what". They had successfully rifled through the Argentinian containers that lined the roads around Stanley and their haul included several thousand cigarettes, tins of cooked beef, packets of sweets and many other goodies as well as, Monster's recollection notwithstanding, a good number of the small whiskey bottles that came out of the Argentinean ration packs.

It must be admitted that other forms of foraging also took place. One of the first tasks the Flight undertook after the Argentinean surrender was on 15th June, when we were approached furtively by two former members of NP8901, who had been at Moody Brook Camp when the Argentineans invaded. They told Will Scott that they knew where their unit's quartermaster had hidden a years' supply of booze, and convinced Will it was worth a trip to recover it. Will and Ken, with this dodgy pair embarked, set out that evening, armed with a flashlight, spade, an 'X marks the spot' map, and an underslung load net. Arriving at Moody Brook the two passengers set off from the aircraft on foot but came back, a short while later, crestfallen, and empty handed. They said that the stock had all gone and surmised that the Argentineans had looted it. Somewhat disgruntled, the four recovered to Teal Inlet; there was to be no party that night. However, the story does not end there. Months later, back in Arbroath, Will was invited for dinner by Ian Gardiner, who had been a company commander in 45 Commando during the Campaign. Chatting amiably about the post conflict stage, Will asked Ian where his company had been accommodated, Ian replied that they had requisitioned some houses on the edge of Port Stanley and that every night they had a huge quantity of booze to drink. Ian had no idea where the booze had come from. Will asked him if he had had any of the NP8901 team with him and he said 'Yes, the NP8901 storeman had been seconded to his company'. Will knew straightaway where the booze supply had come from and was quietly pleased that, at least, it had not ended up in Argentinean hands!

On another occasion, JC and I landed at one of the old gun positions, behind Mount Kent and gathered up about forty shell cases, allowing most of the flight to go home with some 'allowable' trophies of war! Meanwhile, Bill O'Brien had taken Gen Moore out to West Falkland to do a tour of 40 Commando locations.

Last stop Fox Bay where, during a lull, I was invited by one of the sentries into a big barn which was packed with Argentinian small arms of every calibre and function. 'Take what you like' he said with a wink, 'I have'. Ten minutes later I was the proud possessor of an M1911, Colt Government 45, complete with spare mags and holster!

On 22nd June, we were told to fire off any rockets remaining loaded in the aircraft. A sensible idea, much safer and easier than unloading ordnance that had been left in the pods for some time in difficult environmental conditions. One of Angus Horswill' s last flights in the Falklands, was to fire off the remaining SNEBs in CM's pods into a small island just to the north of Teal Inlet:

The results were totally unimpressive. I think we were all glad we'd never had to use them in anger. The firings went quite well but not a shot in anger had been fired from a Gazelle during the campaign and it was clear from this exercise that the most we could have hoped from them was to distract an opponent, with ordinance coming in their general direction and thus complicating their targeting.

On the 23rd June, we spent our last night in the Falkland's back on our old friend and comforter, Sir Percival. All the aircraft had been flown to the MV Elk to be transported home and were now grounded. No surprise really, the aircraft had been overworked and overstressed and most would probably have not been deemed airworthy under any normal circumstances. The LAD had been using every trick from the BDR handbook to keep them going. Bill O'Brien recalls: "It was a sombre evening, but an old projector cranked out 'For Your Eyes Only'; there was a bit to drink and no flying the next day".

Aboard the Prize Ship

Most of 3 Commando Brigade was to travel back to UK on the SS Canberra whilst the Paras embarked on the SS Norland, for transit to Ascension Island, from where they were to be flown the rest of the way home. 5 Brigade was to remain on the Islands, until a new garrison could be established. Embarking on SS Canberra for a cruise class return to Blighty, it was to be the first time the whole Squadron had been collocated since the adventure began.

However, our first challenge was to get aboard. We were being transferred from Sir Percival on a prize ship, an Argentinian tug with only one working screw, captained by an unfortunate, young, naval, Sub-Lieutenant. There was a companionway rigged down the side of Canberra, by means of which we were to embark. On his first attempt, our 'prize captain' missed the companion way completely; on the second he nearly destroyed it, as the tug bounced off the fenders that had wisely been lowered. At this point, a gnarly old RN Captain lent over the Canberra's bridge wing and using a loud hailer, to the intense embarrassment of the Sub-Lieutenant said, "Best that you heave-to and we'll manoeuvre to you!". Happily, the poor soul made it on the third attempt!

All together for the first time, the Squadron partied hard, we had taken a more than proportional share of casualties among the aircrew and having been involved in every action of the Campaign, all the Brigade's units had become familiar with us. Many a good night was had as the Squadron's officers gathered around a piano in the Crow's Nest Bar (Captain Paul Bancroft was our pianist), repeatedly singing the few crass rugby songs we all knew and probably annoying everyone else.

Elsewhere on the ship, as Angus Horswill recalls:

After the events of the previous twelve weeks, being on the Canberra presented some sort of alternate reality. Apparently, when the ship had been taken up from trade, she had been midway through a cruise. Because of the rush to get her away, there had been insufficient time to de-store, so Naval rations had been loaded on top of the normal cruise fare. Apparently, when the purser had asked the MoD how long he could expect to be at sea before a replenishment, he had been told that they didn't know and he should make his food stocks last as long as possible. When we embarked, all the naval rations had come to an end and we were to be fed on cruise food. Because most of it was coming to the end of its "eat by" date, what wasn't consumed would be sent to the tip on return to the UK. We ate like kings to the extent that, after a couple of days, most of us actually cut down to two meals a day as it was too much.

As an example, SS Canberra laid on a 'crossing the line' dinner with a 'special menu' for the embarked force's officers.

Bill O'Brien remembers that:

The accommodation and food were great and, apart from daily PT and the odd parade, there was little by way of military routine for the first couple of weeks. CSE shows came onboard as we passed the Canaries and did their best to entertain 3,500 Marines returning from war but mainly, we drank a lot, spun 'dits[37]', said a prayer for our wounded, and remembered our dead.

In retrospect, it was the best possible way for us to return home. Two weeks to unwind from the tensions of everyday combat and surviving, with only our immediate comrades for company. The embarked RM Band, who had themselves been involved in

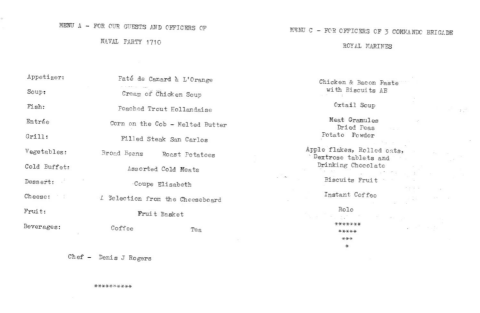

MENU A - FOR OUR GUESTS AND OFFICERS OF NAVAL PARTY 1710		MENU C - FOR OFFICERS OF 3 COMMANDO BRIGADE ROYAL MARINES
Appetizer:	Paté de Canard à L'Orange	Chicken & Bacon Paste with Biscuits AB
Soup:	Cream of Chicken Soup	
Fish:	Poached Trout Hollandaise	Oxtail Soup
Entrée	Corn on the Cob - Melted Butter	Meat Granules Dried Peas
Grill:	Filled Steak San Carlos	Potato Powder
Vegetables:	Broad Beans Roast Potatoes	Apple flakes, Rolled oats, Dextrose tablets and
Cold Buffet:	Assorted Cold Meats	Drinking Chocolate
Dessert:	Coupe Elisabeth	Biscuits Fruit
Cheese:	A Selection from the Cheeseboard	Instant Coffee
Fruit:	Fruit Basket	Rolo
Beverages:	Coffee Tea	******* ***** *** *

Chef - Denis J Rogers

****

Canberra's Crossing the Line Dinner Menu

---

[37] Dit: Any written (or spoken) account of an incident or event in a sailor's life... (Jolly 1999 p 136)

combat, contributing to our medical support, provided musical entertainment during the voyage and a memorable concert on the open deck of SS Canberra, the evening before we berthed in Southampton.

Over the last few days, Routine Orders had been ominously pointing out that 'individuals found in possession of 'Trophies of War' when processed through customs - to which all on board would be subject – would be charged and forgo their leave. As we approached Southampton, Bill O'Brien was chatting with mates on the starboard side main deck;

Above the normal sounds of engine and passing sea, we heard distinctive splashes. I looked over the side and saw that everyone who had ignored or kept their nerve against the 'Trophies of War' directive had undergone a change of heart at the last minute and everything from pistols to MGs was being ditched through scuttles or anywhere that discreet access could be found. I lost my bottle too and said goodbye to my government colt. Later I discovered that even the earliest through the arrival sheds were simply waved past the Customs desks, nothing and nobody was checked and by the time we got to the sheds there was only tumbleweed blowing through.

As we approached the UK coast off Falmouth on 11th July, we began to get an inkling of the welcome that awaited us. We did not really have access to news so, the euphoria taking place throughout Britain was rather remote; most of us just thought it would be nice to get home. Throughout this final passage, we were buzzed by airplanes and helicopters, and speed boats came out from the south coast to sail next to us.

Approaching Southampton

Arrival

The day was bright, warm, and sunny as Canberra steamed up the Solent. That morning Canberra treated us to a steak breakfast and the buzz went around to look outside. We were entering the eastern Solent and the water around us was a mass of small boats, it was all great fun, girls waving their bikini tops at us and the lads collectively singing 'Rule Britannia' and thumping the side of the boat at the same time. We were visited by HRH Prince Charles and our own Commandant General, then treated to a Red Arrows fly past before docking. The Ship's berthing area was awash with relatives and friends who had been waiting patiently for our arrival.

It was for us a magnificent welcome home but an event also tinged with sadness, not only for the friends we had lost who could not share with us this proud moment but also, we faced the parting of the brotherhood as we prepared to head our separate ways and back to the realities of life at home. We had no aircraft or equipment, it was all on other, slower ships, so we were heading home, straight on leave, some to Arbroath and some to the West Country. Monster reflected:

that was the end of M Flt, we never really had a disbanding run ashore. I can't remember if I went back to Arbroath but all the kit that had gone south went straight to [the Squadron's base at] Coypool.

Those bound for Arbroath were first to disembark, together with 45 Cdo. As they left the customs shed JC was greeted by my in-laws who had travelled from Hastings to welcome me coming off the Canberra. However, time was short and all the Arbroath contingent were swiftly loaded on to the waiting coaches and driven to Southampton airport, through the Emergency gates and straight to the back of waiting RAF Hercules. Swift load and off we went straight to RAF Leuchars.

Those of us with homes in the West Country joined our families on the quayside before traveling in a fleet of coaches on the most extraordinary journey of my life, with crowds gathered on every bridge and every town and village high street between Southampton and Plymouth, cheering us on our way. My wife was there with the son I had never seen as was Alyson Priest who introduced Ken to his now 12-month-old daughter!

Meanwhile the Arbroath contingent was experiencing what JC recalls as "his swiftest journey ever in the Corps":

[At RAF Leuchars,] another swift unload on to new coaches and another swift departure toward Dundee and finally Arbroath. We arrived in Arbroath as the first coaches arrived in Plymouth. As with the Southern contingent the route was thronged with crowds welcoming us back, Arbroath was bedlam with the roads and streets overflowing with flags, banners, and crowds of well-wishers. Arrival at Condor was amazing with excited families, children, loved ones, more banners and flags all rushing to greet us off the coaches. This was tinged with sadness for our colleagues who never made it home.

As Charlie Walker put it simply, it was "good to get up to Arbroath to see and enjoy all the effort put in by the folk at home".

Epilogue

Montfortebeek Flight's efforts were recognised with a Distinguished Flying Medal (DFM) for Bill O'Brien, a Mention in Dispatches (MiD) for me and a CinC's Commendation for Will Scott, though sadly, my attempt to get some recognition for the LAD failed. However, as Monster had reflected, M Flight effectively disbanded as we disembarked in Southampton, straight to our homes and leave, some of us never to return to Arbroath. Angus Horswill continued with his interrupted return to the Army, whilst JC went straight from leave to another Royal Marine unit, prior to an Army Pilot's course and an exchange tour with the Army Air Corps. On the passage home, I had been told that I would be going straight on a Lynx Conversion course and taking over B Flight from Jeff Niblett, as it re-equipped with six of the new TOW missile armed Westland Lynx helicopters. Bill O'Brien was also selected for the course. The sad task of closing what remained of the Flight in Arbroath and unceremoniously transferring the remaining people and equipment to Plymouth, to be integrated into other flights, fell to Will Scott. However, between them, they managed to ensure that M Flt's final departure from Arbroath did not go entirely unmarked…

Globe and Laurel Sep/Oct 1982 Edition

Although most of us initially took on new roles in the Squadron, the fellowship was broken; we gradually drifted our separate ways and, with a few exceptions, lost touch.

The occasional Squadron reunions organised by Peter Cameron and John Gilbert, who had been Peter's Squadron Sergeant Major, have done much to keep some of us in touch and I hope that memories stirred by this book may draw in more.

Wearied by Age – at the Squadron 35th Reunion
Nick Pounds, Bill Obrien, Will Scott, Ken Priest, Dolly Drummond

Just like the old days… Will Scott and Ken Priest

They were heady days we shared back in 1982 and it has been good to get back in touch and to share memories with some of my comrades in arms at the time. There were good times, bad times, easy times, hard times, frustrating times, frightening times and funny times. Our memories and perspectives of each part of the story vary depending on our role within the Flight but I believe that we all look back with fondness on a job well done as a 'Small Cog' in a historic enterprise.